Susan Solloway
290 Northpoint Ave
Huntington, IN  46750-8452

W9-DIJ-250

# Salvation

WHAT EVERY CATHOLIC SHOULD KNOW

# Salvation

**WHAT EVERY CATHOLIC SHOULD KNOW**

Michael Patrick Barber

*Foreword by Brant Pitre*

IGNATIUS PRESS
San Francisco

AUGUSTINE INSTITUTE
Greenwood Village, CO

**Ignatius Press**
San Francisco, CA

**Augustine Institute**
Greenwood Village, CO

Cover Design: Ben Dybas

©2019 Ignatius Press, San Francisco,
and the Augustine Institute, Greenwood Village, CO
All rights reserved
ISBN 978-1-7335221-8-2 (pbk)
ISBN 978-1-7338598-0-6 (hbk)
Library of Congress Control Number 2019935228

Printed in Canada ∞

*To Kim*

# Contents

# by Brant Pitre

*Why did God become man?* In other words, what was the *reason* for the Incarnation? If you had to answer this question with one word, what would you say?

Thankfully, if you're Catholic, you don't have to look far for the answer. You can simply turn to the words of the Nicene Creed, which sum up the essential points of the Christian faith. Every Sunday at Mass, Catholics throughout the world confess that Jesus Christ, the Son of God, came down from heaven "for us men and *for our salvation*."

Obviously, if the Church requires Catholics to recite these Sunday after Sunday, they must be important. But what do they mean? What exactly is "salvation"?

Although I've been a Catholic all of my life, I must confess that I can count on one hand the number of homilies I remember that were focused on "salvation" or being "saved." For whatever reason, Catholics nowadays often just don't talk that way—even though Jesus himself declared that he came "to seek and *to save* the lost" (Luke 19:10). By contrast, when I was a teenager, my future wife, Elizabeth, was Southern Baptist, and I used to go to services with her on occasion. In her church, it seemed as if almost *every* sermon was about "being saved." Virtually every Sunday, the "gospel" of the forgiveness of sins through the death of Jesus Christ would be proclaimed, and those who were not yet believers would be invited to come and receive the gift of "salvation."

Now, there's an old saying of Aristotle: "Nature abhors a vacuum." As a Bible professor, I sometimes like to alter it slightly: "*Theology* abhors a vacuum." What I mean by this is that whenever any aspect of the Catholic faith starts to be neglected, what remains in the minds and the hearts of ordinary Catholics is not just a "blank space." Instead, errors that get picked up here and there along the way inevitably rush in to fill the void. The end result is people who have wrong ideas about what salvation is and how it works. Oftentimes, many Catholics (and I include myself in this) don't even know that what they believe salvation is contradicts the Church's teachings.

In his fantastic book, *Salvation: What Every Catholic Should Know*, Dr. Michael Barber takes the reader on a guided tour into the world of what theologians refer to as *soteriology*: the doctrine of "salvation" (Greek *sotēria*). The end result is a truly brilliant corrective to the many misunderstandings regarding salvation that have found their way into the minds and hearts of many Christians, including many Catholics. With writing that is both readable and charitable, Dr. Barber shows over and over again what salvation is *not*: it is not "self-help" (as in ancient Pelagianism and modern Therapeutic Deism); not mere "fire insurance" (as in Fundamentalism); not "without cost" (as in the "Health and Wealth Gospel" preached by certain televangelists); not just "personal" (as in Individualism); not just a "legal transaction," a "spectator sport," or simply a "moment" (as in some forms of Protestantism); it is not "inevitable" (as in Universalism); nor is it just about the future (as in some forms of Dispensationalism). Most important of all—and as we all need to be reminded on a regular basis— salvation is not just for "other people." But that's not all. Even more importantly, Barber shows us what the Bible says salvation *is*. According to Scripture, salvation is returning to the Father; knowing the Lord; a revelation of divine love; an unmerited gift of righteousness that actually transforms us; a participation in the passion, death, and resurrection of Jesus Christ, and, above all, entering into the very life of the blessed Trinity: the Father, the Son, and the Holy Spirit. At every step, Barber makes a compelling case that this Catholic view of salvation is thoroughly and incontrovertibly *biblical*. While some discussions of salvation—especially the centuries-old debate between Protestants and Catholics over justification, faith, and works—can quickly veer off into technical philosophical and theological debates, this book makes an incredibly complex topic incredibly clear by keeping our eyes focused on what the Bible itself has to say about the subject.

In short, Dr. Barber has given us all a very precious gift: a book that shows both what Jesus Christ came into this world to save us *from* and, equally important, what he came to save us *for*.

# What Is Salvation?

For I am not ashamed of the gospel: it is the power of God for salvation to every one who has faith . . .
—Romans 1:16[1]

Everything comes from love. All is ordained for the salvation of man. God does nothing without this goal in mind.
—St. Catherine of Siena,
cited in *Catechism of the Catholic Church* §313[2]

*Are you saved?*

The first time someone asked me this question I was a teenager. The context of the conversation was a memorable one. My parents had taken me and my five siblings on a trip to Northern California as part of a family vacation. We piled into a van, left our home in Southern California, and spent hours on the road. The journey took us on along a scenic route. We saw rugged mountains, shimmering lakes, and forested regions.

You might expect me to say that the remarkable vistas were the highlight of the trip. To be honest, I barely remember any of them. Instead, my clearest memory from that vacation was a brief exchange I had in the hotel lobby. I somehow ended up

---

1    Unless otherwise noted, all biblical translations are taken from the Revised Standard Version Catholic Edition (RSV-CE). Throughout the book, emphases added to quotes are author's own.
2    St. Catherine of Siena, *Dialogue on Providence*, chapter IV, 138.

getting involved in a conversation about music with a group of kids my age. That is when things took an interesting turn.

### Salvation: Past or Future?

We were all naming our favorite musical artists when someone mentioned a singer who is well known in the Christian music industry. No one in our group recognized the name—except for me. My father had always enjoyed contemporary Christian music, and so I was familiar with the genre. When I seconded the kid's endorsement, he was pleasantly surprised. He did not expect anyone to recognize the singer. It seemed like we had just connected on a new level. I suppose I should have seen what was coming next, but I did not.

The boy turned to me and asked, "Are you saved?"

I suddenly felt like a deer in the headlights. The question caught me completely off guard. Thankfully, at that precise moment some of the other members of the group interrupted, offering their own musical recommendations. Everyone else seemed uninterested in the matter of my salvation. Nevertheless, from the look on his face I could tell that the guy who had raised the issue was not going to drop the question. It was going to come back up.

As the others talked, I recall being slightly put off by his question. Was I *saved?* I assumed he was asking me if I was going to hell. "Look," I almost responded, "I am a good guy. I go to church regularly. Why would you even ask me that?"

But I also remember being perplexed. My thoughts ran something like this: "If salvation is about getting out of hell and going to heaven, shouldn't the question be, 'Do you think you *will* be saved?'"

I would later learn that my instincts were not entirely correct. While the New Testament does talk about salvation as a future event, it also describes it as something that has already occurred in the life of the believer. On the one hand, speaking of the day of judgment, Paul says believers "*will be* saved"

(1 Corinthians 3:15). On the other, the New Testament writers also indicate that salvation is an event that has already taken place in the life of the believer. For instance, in Titus 3:5 we are told that Christ "saved us . . . by the washing of regeneration and renewal in the Holy Spirit." Yet, as a young Catholic, I had never thought about salvation as involving an event that took place in the past.

When the discussion about music died down, I was put on the spot again—"Are you saved?" he asked a second time. With a hint of protest in my voice, I responded, "Of course!" He seemed pleased with my answer. But I was not.

I knew I had only told him what he wanted to hear. Our conversation ended, and we went our separate ways. Still, the question stuck with me. Long after we had returned from our trip, I was still thinking about it. In a certain sense, I do not think I have ever stopped thinking about it. This is the book I wish I had read prior to being asked, "Are you saved?" It is primarily written for Catholics, though it is my hope that non-Catholic Christians will profit from reading it as well.

### Rethinking "Salvation"

I have discovered that many Catholics can relate to my experience. As Catholics we are very familiar with the language of "salvation." We know it is important. In fact, at every Sunday Mass we proclaim our faith in Christ by affirming the Creed, which states, *"for our salvation* he came down from heaven." We know that the Son of God became man *to save us.* We even call him the *Savior.*

As Catholics, we think we know what being saved means—until we are asked about it. Only then do many of us come to realize how little we have actually reflected on what salvation really involves. We even tend to substitute other phrases for "salvation." When I told a Catholic friend that I was writing a book about salvation, his immediate reaction was: "Why not just call it *How to Get to Heaven?*" I had to laugh. *That* is precisely my point. Rarely—if *ever*!—do we Catholics talk to another about being "saved."

Indeed, to pious Catholic ears, it almost sounds "un-Catholic" to use the language of being "saved." If a stranger were to show up in the parish hall after Sunday Mass and start talking about being "saved," I suspect some parishioners might even wonder if he was a non-Catholic Christian who was just visiting the parish.

Yet why should Catholics be reticent about being *saved?* We call Jesus the *Savior.* If that matters to us, we should want to know what salvation really entails.

Furthermore, consider the following: if someone told you that they loved you and then added that they did not really care to know much about you, would you not start to wonder if that person's love for you was truly genuine? Is this not, however, our attitude towards Jesus if we remain uninterested in the topic of salvation? How can we profess a belief in a *Savior,* but fail to care about what this means?

The truth is, my understanding of salvation as a Catholic teenager was woefully simplistic. That was a problem. And it was not just a problem because it left me ill-equipped to *explain* my faith. Being ignorant of the meaning of salvation meant that I did not know what *I* believed. And if we do not know what we believe as Catholics, how can we live our faith?

### Salvation as Rethinking

This brings me to one of the important lessons I hope readers will take away from this book: bad theology always leads to difficulties in one's spiritual life. This a truth that is necessary to underscore. Theology is essential for the Church's pastoral mission and life of faith. Sadly, many fail to appreciate this. Theology is often viewed merely as a form of Catholic trivia. It is even becoming increasingly common to suggest that theology is somehow antithetical to spirituality or to pastoral concerns.

I once knew a priest who often expressed this idea in his homilies. "Don't get distracted by all that fancy theology," he would state in a charming, northeastern accent. "All that matters is that you have Jesus in your heart."

Having Jesus in your heart *is* important; on that point, I fully agree. But it is not simply enough to love the Lord with all one's heart. When Jesus is asked what the greatest commandment is, he responds, "You shall love the Lord your God with all your heart, and with all your soul, *and with all your mind.*" (Matthew 22:37).

Did you catch that? Loving the Lord with our *minds* is indispensable. One cannot be Jesus's disciple and ignore this aspect of his teaching. In fact, the Greek word "disciple" (*mathētēs*) literally means "student." As a professor, I like to remind my students what being a student involves—students must *study.* If we are called to be Jesus's disciples, we are also called to grow constantly in understanding our faith.

Of course, I am *not* suggesting that every believer needs to earn academic degrees in theology. Most of the greatest saints in Church history never did. Nonetheless, you cannot be truly committed to following Jesus and refuse to think about what that entails. St. Paul writes, ". . . be transformed by the renewal of your mind" (Romans 12:2). For Paul, spiritual transformation comes, in part, by being transformed in one's *thinking.*

### *The Bible and Catholic Tradition*
My principal aim in this book will be to unpack what the New Testament teaches about salvation in Christ. In this, I seek to follow the official teaching of the Second Vatican Council, which insists that "the soul of sacred theology" should be "the study of the sacred page," that is, Scripture.[3]

---

3   Vatican II, *Dei Verbum* ["The Word of God"], §24.

While the arguments here are rooted in careful scholarship, I have kept the main text free of technical jargon. For those interested in the scholarly work that supports my explanations of Scripture, I have provided footnotes. These contain references to more technical pieces I have written as well as to works by other academics.[4] But let me be clear: the notes are not necessary for the general reader. This is a book for *anyone* who wants to know what salvation in Christ means.

In reflecting on Scripture's teaching, we not only draw from the insights of contemporary scholars, but also wish to learn from the wisdom of the Church's tradition. To this end, I will frequently cite the fathers and doctors of the Church. In addition, I will have frequent recourse to the *Catechism of the Catholic Church* (which will simply be referred to as "the *Catechism*"). This work should not be confused with other "catechisms," such as the *Baltimore Catechism*. The *Catechism* is not written to be read by children. It was first published by Pope John Paul II and brings together Scripture's teaching with various witnesses of Catholic tradition. Since it was published, more recent popes— Pope Benedict XVI and Pope Francis—have continued to cite it as an official summary of Catholic teaching.[5]

G. K. Chesterton talked about the importance of tradition this way:

> Tradition means giving votes to the most obscure of all classes, our ancestors. It is the democracy of the dead. Tradition refuses to submit to the small and arrogant oligarchy of those who merely happen to be walking about. . . . Democracy tells us not to

---

4    See, especially, the more detailed exegetical analysis found in Brant Pitre, Michael P. Barber, and John A. Kincaid, *Paul, A New Covenant Jew* (Grand Rapids: Eerdmans, 2019). In addition, see my contributions in Alan Stanley, ed., *Four Views on the Role of Works at the Final Judgment* with James D.G. Dunn et al (Grand Rapids: Zondervan, 2013).

5    Benedict XVI, *Porta Fidei* ["Door of Faith"], §11; Francis, Address to Participants in the Meeting Promoted by the Pontifical Council for Promoting the New Evangelization (October 11, 2017).

neglect a good man's opinion . . . tradition asks us not to neglect a good man's opinion, even if he is our father.[6]

By reading Scripture in light of the Church's tradition, we recognize the way the Spirit has guided past generations in their meditation on Scripture. Tradition refuses to ignore their encounter with the Lord in the Bible.

Each chapter, then, will begin with two brief quotations. The first is taken from the Bible. This underscores that our whole discussion of salvation will be rooted in biblical teaching. The second quotation will come from the *Catechism*. This is not meant to imply that the *Catechism* is somehow on the same level as Scripture. Far from it! Rather, one of my goals throughout this book is to explain how the Catholic understanding of salvation flows from a thoughtful reading of the Bible that seeks to preserve its message.[7]

### *The Savior in the New Testament*

Finally, let me offer two simple caveats upfront. First, in the Bible, God's saving work takes various forms. I cannot discuss all of them here. In this book we will be focusing in particular on *Jesus's* work of salvation. As a result, though we will also draw from the Old Testament, the New Testament will be emphasized in our discussion.

Second, this book is not intended to be a complete account of the New Testament's teaching about salvation. The treatment here is ordered towards a reflection on spirituality. Some New Testament books will receive little to no attention. Moreover, when I refer to "the New Testament's teaching" or use similar language, I do not mean to imply that all the inspired authors[8]

---

6    G. K. Chesterton, *Orthodoxy* (New York: John Lane Company, 1908), 85.

7    Vatican II, *Dei Verbum*, §10.

8    In this book I cannot discuss all the issues relating to the authorship of the various New Testament books. Here, following scholarly convention, I refer to them using their traditional titles without prejudice to such discussions.

speak of salvation in precisely the same way. Each of their presentations has distinctive nuances. That being said, there is substantial agreement among them on what salvation entails. It is not wrong, then, to speak in broad terms about an overall New Testament teaching about salvation.

In particular, the New Testament writers affirm that "salvation" comes through Christ. When Joseph is instructed in a dream to take Mary as his wife, he is also told what name to give the Messiah: "*. . . you shall call his name Jesus, for he will save his people from their sins*" (Matthew 1:21). "Jesus" is a translation of the Hebrew name "Yehoshua" ("Joshua"), which, as the *Catechism* explains, means "the LORD saves" (§430).[9] To misunderstand salvation is to fail to understand fully who the Savior is. It is my hope that this book will give readers not only a better understanding of what salvation is, but a deeper love *for the Savior himself.*

With that in mind we now turn to our first chapter, which seeks to counter a common misconception about the nature of salvation, namely, that salvation is essentially about "self-help."

---

9    See Ben F. Meyer, "Jesus," in *Anchor Bible Dictionary*, 6 vols. (New York: Doubleday, 1992), 3:773.

# 1

# Not Self-Help

For by grace you have been saved through faith; and
this is not your own doing, it is the gift of God—not
because of works, lest any man should boast.

—Ephesians 2:8–9

Our salvation flows from God's initiative of love for us . . .

—*Catechism of the Catholic Church* §620

Walk into almost any bookstore these days and you will likely
discover a section devoted to a relatively new, yet wildly popular,
genre: "self-help." Most of the books found in this aisle have
one essential premise: the problems you struggle with can be
solved if you follow the right advice. With the right motivation,
personal resolve, and positive thinking, you can learn how to
become "a better you."

The Bible cannot be found in this section of the bookstore,
and for good reason. The New Testament authors insist one
cannot be saved by "self-help." According to St. Paul—the man
Church tradition refers to as "the Apostle"—doing the right
thing is not merely difficult, but *impossible*: "For I do not do
what I want, but I do the very thing I hate. . . . I can will what is
right, but *I cannot do it*. For I do not do the good I want, but the
evil I do not want is what I do (Romans 7:15, 18–19).

There is also another reason why being saved cannot be
realized through self-help. St. Paul goes on to say that salvation

is about much more than just becoming "a better you." To be saved is to be united to God in Christ and to be "conformed to the image of his Son" (Romans 8:29).

If becoming like Christ sounds "difficult," you are being too optimistic. If this sounds "challenging," you are missing the point. Humanly speaking, what God calls us to is completely beyond our reach. It is truly *impossible.*

The good thing is, as Jesus reminds us, "What is impossible with men is possible with God" (Luke 18:27). God makes the impossible possible by his assistance. To make this point the New Testament authors use a critically important word: grace.

## GRACE AS GOD'S MERCIFUL GIFT

Virtually all Christians affirm that grace is central to the Gospel message. Classic hymns like "Amazing Grace" celebrate grace's vital role in the Christian life. But what does the word "grace" actually mean? As we shall see, the word is crucial for understanding the Gospel message.

### Grace as a Gift

In the letter to the Ephesians we read: "For by grace you have been saved through faith; and this is not your own doing, it is the gift of God" (Ephesians 2:8). It is no coincidence that grace is here spoken of as a "gift." John Barclay, an Anglican New Testament scholar, has recently been doing groundbreaking scholarship, in which he analyzes the way Paul's teaching about grace relates to gift-giving in the ancient world.[1] Here I will briefly explain some of his important insights.

---

1     See Barclay, *Paul and the Gift* (Grand Rapids: Eerdmans, 2015). For a discussion of "grace" in the Johannine literature that interacts with Barclay's contribution, see Francis J. Moloney, *Johannine Studies*, 1975–2017 (Tübingen: Mohr Siebeck, 2017), 283–305.

The Greek word that is usually translated "grace" is *charis*. It is frequently used in Greek literature to refer to a "gift." When Paul talks about "the grace [*charis*] of God" (Galatians 2:21), his meaning would have been fairly straightforward to his original Greek-speaking audiences—"the grace of God" meant "the gift of God." Paul's teaching about "grace" is, at its root, about God's *gift* to humanity which is made available in Christ.

Gifts played a vital role in ancient society. They established, cemented, and defined relationships. Ancient gift-giving involved a complex system of etiquette. Those who received gifts understood that they were under a special obligation to reciprocate, that is, to make a return-gift. The ancient Roman author Seneca compares gift-giving to a game of catch, which requires a continuous back-and-forth exchange. As Barclay puts it, the goal was "to keep the ball (the gift) continually circulating back and forth."[2]

The fact that gifts came with expectations could, of course, lead to difficulties. This was especially the case when gifts were exchanged between parties of different economic and social classes. To ensure that all things went smoothly, the two parties would often enter into delicate negotiations regarding how the recipient would reciprocate.

Because gift-giving was aimed at initiating a circle of reciprocity, rich benefactors had a responsibility to find worthy recipients. Financial gifts were only to be bestowed on those who would keep the circle of giving in motion. To give indiscriminately was viewed as foolish, even disreputable.

Ancient perspectives on gift-giving help us better understand Paul's teaching about God's grace. According to Paul, God is the perfect giver. The Father bestows on humanity the greatest gift possible, namely, his own Son. The "gift" is not just "power" or "favor" but *Christ himself.* In fact, Christ

---

2  See Barclay, *Paul and the Gift*, 46.

is also the giver for Paul, since he makes a gift of *himself*. In Galatians, we read, "*Grace* to you and peace from God the Father and our Lord Jesus Christ, who *gave himself* for our sins to deliver us from the present evil age" (Galatians 1:3–4). The gift of God—grace—is here inseparable from Christ's act of self-giving on the cross.

Yet, according to the Apostle, the divine gift made available in Christ is bestowed in a truly astonishing way: it is given to the *unworthy*. Paul writes: "While we were yet helpless, at the right time Christ died for the ungodly. . . . But God shows his love for us in that while we were yet sinners Christ died for us" (Romans 5:6, 8). Christians are saved by Christ's act of life-giving love, which he offered *while we were still sinners*. Paul even says Christ died for us while we were God's "enemies" (Romans 5:10).

The Apostle further stresses the generosity of God by saying, ". . . where sin increased, grace abounded all the more" (Romans 5:20). Therefore, instead of turning away from sinful humanity, God does just the opposite. The more humanity retreats from God, the more God comes after us.

Grace is given to those who are in sin. Our sin does not prevent the Lord from loving us.

### Jesus's Merciful Search for the Lost

Nonetheless, it is necessary to stress that, according to the Gospels, Jesus does not commend sinners *for their sins*. Jesus comes to bring repentance. Luke illustrates this point by telling us about an encounter Jesus had with a tax collector named Zacchaeus.

In Luke 19, Jesus enters the city of Jericho and Zacchaeus, a short man, is unable to catch a glimpse of him. To get a better view, Zacchaeus climbs up a sycamore tree. Jesus notices him there and, to the chagrin of the crowds, announces: "Zacchaeus, make haste and come down; for I must stay at your house today" (Luke 19:5). This provokes scandal. Luke tells us, ". . . they all murmured, 'He has gone in to be the guest of a man who is a sinner'" (Luke 19:7).

Tax collectors were Jews who had betrayed their own people. They were in league with the Romans, the pagan empire that had conquered Judea. Roman oppression was cruel and often involved horrific brutality. As one source explains, "The [Roman] army lived off the occupied country, pilfering its natural resources, enslaving members of its population, raping women and generally terrorizing the populace."[3]

Jews who became tax collectors, therefore, were especially despised. They aligned themselves with the vile Romans, betrayed their own people, and did so for personal profit. They were also known for being dishonest. Jesus assumes their despised status in various places in the Gospels. For instance, in Matthew's Gospel, Jesus asks, "For if you love those who love you, what reward have you? *Do not even the tax collectors do the same?*" (Matthew 5:46).

Yet Jesus's desire to dine with the man should not be interpreted as indicating that he took a permissive attitude towards sin. Rather, the overall narrative suggests that Jesus's act is aimed at leading the tax collector to a genuine conversion. We go on to read:

> And Zacchaeus stood and said to the Lord, "Behold, Lord, the half of my goods I give to the poor; and if I have defrauded any one of anything, I restore it fourfold." And Jesus said to him, "*Today salvation has come to this house*, since he also is a son of Abraham. For *the Son of man came to seek and to save the lost.*" (Luke 19:8–10)

---

3    W. J. Heard and K. Yamazaki-Ransom, "Revolutionary Movements," in *Dictionary of Jesus and the Gospels*, Second Edition, eds. Jeannine K. Brown and Nicholas Perrin (Downers Grove: IVP Academic, 2013), 789.

Jesus dines with Zacchaeus as part of his stated mission: "to seek and save the lost." Notice that Jesus is not simply the "Savior," but that he also reveals himself as "Seeker." He is actively searching for those in need of salvation. Jesus dines with Zacchaeus to change him.

Jesus succeeds in his mission. The tax collector pledges to make amends for his wrong doing. Saving the lost is not only about associating with them. Jesus's announcement of salvation follows Zacchaeus's pledge to set right the things he has done wrong. Salvation is not simply about confession, it also involves transformation and restitution.

Moreover, Zacchaeus plans to correct his wrongdoing in a remarkable way. Just as Jesus exceeds Zacchaeus's expectations by coming to his house, Zacchaeus's response likewise goes beyond what one might have anticipated from him. Not only does Zacchaeus promise to restore whatever he has stolen, he states that he will do so *fourfold*—he will give back four times whatever he has taken.

Jesus's extravagant mercy, then, is aimed at producing prodigious repentance. This idea is expressed in another story in Luke's Gospel: the account of a sinful woman who anoints Jesus.

### He Who Is Forgiven Little, Loves Little

In Luke 7, Jesus is sitting at table in the house of a Pharisee named Simon. There he is approached by a woman who is a well-known sinner. Whatever it was that earned her this reputation, Simon is appalled by what Jesus permits her to do: she wets Jesus's feet with her tears, washes them with her hair, and anoints him with expensive ointment. Simon thinks to himself, "If this man were a prophet, he would have known who and what sort of woman this is who is touching him, for she is a sinner" (Luke 7:39).

Jesus demonstrates that he is no ordinary man by revealing his awareness of Simon's inner thoughts. Instead of responding directly to Simon's objection, Jesus tells a parable involving a creditor who has two debtors. In the story, one debtor owes a creditor five hundred denarii, while another owes him fifty. In Jesus's day, a denarius represented the payment one would receive after a full day's worth of work in the fields. From the standpoint of those in first-century Galilee, the first man's debt looks insoluble, yet even the second debtor owes a significant sum. Both, however, are shown mercy and their debts are forgiven. Jesus asks Simon which of the two debtors will love the creditor more (Luke 7:42). Simon replies, "The one, I suppose, to whom he forgave more" (Luke 7:43). Jesus commends him, "You have judged rightly." (Luke 7:43).

Having secured this answer, Jesus indicates that the parable was actually about the sinful woman. He concludes by saying to Simon, "I tell you, her sins, which are many, are forgiven, for she loved much; but he who is forgiven little, loves little." (Luke 7:47). Repentance, then, is linked with *love*. The more honest we are in recognizing our sin, the more we will have to ask to be forgiven. And the more we are forgiven by the Lord, the more we will love him.

## SAVING FAITH AS A GIFT

In all of this, Jesus underscores that salvation is the result of God's mercy. This is revealed when we look more carefully at the story of the sinful woman. The story highlights a key theme found elsewhere in the New Testament: even our response to the Lord is a result of his grace.

### *"Your Faith Has Saved You"*
The Parable of the Two Creditors is meant to explain the reason the woman performed the act of anointing Jesus; she shows great love because she has been forgiven much. At the

end of the scene, Jesus dismisses her by saying, "Your faith has saved you; go in peace" (Luke 7:50). Two dimensions of the episode are important to highlight.

First, it does not seem that the woman suddenly received the gift of faith *because* she anointed Jesus. She anoints him as an expression of her faith. In light of the parable, she is like the debtor who owed much. Her acts are signs of love carried out in *response* to the great mercy that has already been shown to her.[4]

Second, Jesus says she has received *salvation* because of her faith: "Your faith has *saved* you." We will have more to say about the word translated as "faith" (Greek *pistis*) later. For now, it is enough to point out that one dimension of the term translated "faith" is "trust." Later, Luke tells us the Parable of the Pharisee and the Tax Collector, which is addressed to those who "trusted in themselves that they were righteous and despised others" (Luke 18:9). The story teaches that salvation is found in putting faith in the Lord, which means not relying on one's *own* self-generated righteousness. Faith is first and foremost trusting in the Lord's gift of salvation.

Jesus's message here anticipates what we learn later in Ephesians, namely, "by grace you have been saved through faith; and this is not your own doing, it is the gift of God— not because of works, lest any man should boast" (Ephesians 2:8–9). Grace is a "gift" because "it is not your own doing." First and foremost, then, we are not saved by our own actions, but by God's gift and initiative.

To some this might sound "un-Catholic." A common caricature of Catholic teaching is that it rejects the notion of salvation by grace and affirms instead that salvation is simply by works. Nothing could be further from the truth. The *Catechism*

---

4    Though see the fuller treatment in Anthony Giambrone, *Sacramental Charity, Creditor Christology, and the Economy of Salvation* (Tübingen: Mohr Siebeck, 2017), 109–18.

maintains, "Grace is *favor*, the *free and undeserved help* that God gives us to respond to his call to become children of God" (§1996). It goes on to affirm, "Since the initiative belongs to God in the order of grace, *no one can merit the initial grace* of forgiveness and justification, at the beginning of conversion" (§2010). Our good works do have saving value (more on that later), but God's gift of grace is not first given to us because we somehow earn it. God gives the gift of faith *to the unworthy*.

### Faith as the Work of God

In different ways, the New Testament makes the point that faith is the result of God's work. For example, Paul tells the Corinthians, ". . . no one can say 'Jesus is Lord' except by the Holy Spirit" (1 Corinthians 12:3). The Apostle does not mean that a non-believer is unable to pronounce the words "Jesus is Lord." Rather, his point is that without divine assistance no one can say that "Jesus is Lord" *and mean it.*

Similarly, in the Fourth Gospel, Jesus says, "This is *the work of God,* that you *believe* in him whom he has sent" (John 6:29). Those who believe cannot simply attribute their faith to their own insight. Jesus insists, "No one can come to me unless the Father who sent me draws him" (John 6:44).

Matthew's account of Peter's famous confession of faith also emphasizes this truth. After questioning the disciples on what people are saying about him, Jesus puts them on the spot, asking, "But who do you say that I am?" (Matthew 16:15). Peter responds, "You are the Christ, the Son of the living God" (Matthew 16:16). Jesus then explains: "Blessed are you, Simon son of Jonah! For flesh and blood has not revealed this to you, but my Father in heaven" (Matthew 16:17). Jesus assures him that he did not come to the truth because of his own ingenuity or brilliance. Peter's faith has only been made possible by the Father—it is not of "flesh" and "blood," that is, the result of his human powers of perception.

## RETURNING TO THE FATHER

God wants us to be forgiven more than we ourselves want to be forgiven. Yet a major obstacle to this often remains: we fail to believe this to be true. Rather than seeing God as a merciful father, we come to view the Lord as an authoritarian figure who withholds love unless we can earn it. The Bible reveals that this perspective is itself due to sin. Jesus illustrates this in one of his most famous parables, the story often referred to as the Parable of the "Prodigal Son."[5]

### *Forgetting God's Fatherhood*

The Parable of the Prodigal Son begins with an account of a father who has two sons. The younger son asks for his inheritance. Having received it from his father, this son leaves home and squanders all he has on loose living. Eventually, the son hits rock bottom. Jesus explains,

> And when he had spent everything, a great famine arose in that country, and he began to be in want. So he went and joined himself to one of the citizens of that country, who sent him into his fields to feed swine. And he would gladly have fed on the pods that the swine ate; and no one gave him anything. But when he came to himself he said, "How many of my father's hired servants have bread enough and to spare, but I perish here with hunger! I will arise and go to my father, and I will say to him, 'Father, I have sinned against heaven and before you; I am no longer worthy to be called your son; treat me as one of your hired servants.'" (Luke 15:14–19)

Let us focus our attention on a few of the key details here.

First, note that the story moves from sonship to servitude. The young man goes from being the son of a man who had

---

5   For a discussion of debated issues relating to the parable, see Klyne Snodgrass, *Stories with Intent: A Comprehensive Guide to the Parables of Jesus* (Grand Rapids: Eerdmans, 2008), 117–43.

"hired servants" to becoming a servant himself. He realizes that those who have the lowest positions in his father's house are better off than he is.

Second, we are told that "no one gave him anything." This stands in stark contrast to his father, who gave to him freely and liberally. In the original Greek, the father is said to have divided his "life" (Greek *bios*) between his two sons (Luke 15:12). By leaving with his share of his father's goods, the son shirked any responsibility he might one day have to care for his father. The son thinks only of himself. By contrast, the father gave no thought to himself but only to his son.

Third, having lost everything, the young man "came to himself," that is, he came to his senses. In the wider context of Luke 15, Jesus tells two other parables—the lost sheep (Luke 15:4–7) and the lost coin (Luke 15:8–10)—which both illustrate genuine repentance. When Jesus says that the wayward son "came to himself," the point is that the prodigal likewise repents.

Finally, note that the young man despairs of being called his father's son. He resolves to go back and ask to be taken in as merely a servant. His sin causes him to believe that his father could longer love him as his son. This proves incorrect.

### The Forgiving Father

The scene of the son's return home is charged with emotion: Jesus explains, "But while he was yet at a distance, his father saw him and had compassion, and ran and embraced him and kissed him" (Luke 15:20). The son begins the speech he has prepared, saying, "I am no longer worthy to be called your son" (Luke 15:21), but before he can finish everything he planned to say—he never gets to the line "treat me as one of your hired servants"—his father exclaims,

> Bring quickly the best robe, and put it on him; and put a ring on his hand, and shoes on his feet; and bring the fatted calf and kill

> it, and let us eat and make merry; for this my son was dead, and is
> alive again; he was lost, and is found. (Luke 15:22–24)

The father takes the initiative in welcoming his son home.
Even before the son can express contrition, his father is already
running to embrace him.

The story then shifts to the other son who refuses to join
the welcome party. He complains to his father:

> Lo, these many years I have served you, and I *never disobeyed
> your command*; yet you never *gave me a kid*, that I might *make
> merry with my friends*. But when this *son of yours* came, who has
> devoured your living with harlots, you killed for him the fatted
> calf! (Luke 15:29–30)

The older son's words are revealing. He refuses to identify the
younger son as his brother, referring to him instead as "this son
of yours." Likewise, he never calls his dad "father." In short, now
it is the older son who appears cut off from the family. Instead of
relating to his father as a son, the older brother portrays himself
as a servant: ". . . these many years I have *served you*, and I *never
disobeyed your command."* He may have never left the home, but,
like the younger son, he abandons his sonship for slavery. The
disgruntled brother does not want to feast with his family but
instead only desires to "make merry with my friends."

Through it all the father never ceases to identify himself as
the older son's father: "*Son*, you are always with me, and all
that is mine is yours. It was fitting to make merry and be glad,
for this your *brother* was dead, and is alive; he was lost, and
is found" (Luke 15:31–32). The father was eager to reconcile
with his younger son, who once abandoned him. Now he
reaches out in love to his other son. He reminds his son that
he always has a place in the father's house. Although the elder
son fails to identify himself as a member of the family, the
father never stops calling him "son."

As with other parables, the "father" in the story is best seen as an image of God. The story therefore underscores God's unrelenting love for us. According to Scripture, it is only because of sin that we begin to doubt this—sin causes us to forget that God loves us. Instead of remembering God's goodness, we perceive the Lord as hostile or distant to us. Rather than seeing God as our Father we begin to view the Lord as merely our judge.

Yet, while sin encourages us to reduce salvation to a legal matter, the New Testament reminds us that being saved is more than merely escaping divine judgment. If we fail to appreciate this, we will reduce our spiritual life to nothing more than being God's servant and "obeying" God's commandments.

The judge is our Father who never abandons us to ourselves. Without the Lord's help we could never be "saved." What God calls us to is beyond anything we could ever attain on our own. But he gives us the "gift" of his help—he gives us grace. He does this because first and foremost he is not simply lawgiver, but Father. This is why we read: "For by grace you have been saved through faith; and this is not your own doing, it is the gift of God—not because of works, lest any man should boast" (Ephesians 2:8–9). God takes the initiative to save us by his gift.

Indeed, the reason people often neglect the significance of grace is that they fail to fully understand what the goal of salvation is. Contrary to the way many speak, salvation entails much more than merely avoiding the fires of damnation. In the next chapter, then, we will take on this minimalistic view of salvation, which I like to refer to as the "salvation as fire insurance" view.

## 2

# Not Just Fire Insurance

I came that they may have life, and have it abundantly. I am the good shepherd. The good shepherd lays down his life for the sheep. . . . I know my own and my own know me, as the Father knows me and I know the Father . . .
—John 10:10–11, 14

Becoming a disciple of Jesus means accepting the invitation to belong to God's family . . .
—*Catechism of the Catholic Church* §2233

A Catholic friend of mine heard I was writing a book about salvation and told me he was eager to read it. Unfortunately, as we talked, it quickly became apparent that he had a very different book in mind than the one I intended to write.

"If you could just list all the commandments, that would be great," he said. A serious look then came over his face as he added, "After all, the stakes are pretty high. Jesus talks a lot about hell, right?"

Well, yes, Jesus does talk a lot about hell. We will look at that aspect of his teaching in a later chapter. Yet salvation in the New Testament is about much more than merely escaping the fires of eternal damnation. I might also add that salvation entails more than simply getting to heaven. In this chapter, however, let us simply focus on the first point—salvation is more than mere fire insurance.

In the Gospel according to John, Jesus says, "I am the door; if any one enters by me, he will be *saved*, and will go in and out and find pasture" (John 10:9). In the next verse he explains that he has come so that those who believe in him "may have life, and have it abundantly" (John 10:10). What does it mean to have "abundant life"? That is the question we will answer in this chapter.

## THE LAW AND THE LOVE OF GOD

In our modern context, "laws" are essentially understood as regulations and restrictions, rules and prohibitions. For ancient Israel, however, it had a much broader definition. This wider meaning was closely related to the larger biblical story of God's dealings with his people. As we shall see, God's law must not be separated from this story.

### *The Law as More than Rules*
For ancient Jews, the "law" was not simply a list of do's and don'ts. Among other things, the word "law"—in Hebrew, *Torah*—was used to refer to biblical books. In particular, in Jesus's day, the term "law" was applied to what we now recognize as the first five books of the Bible, namely, Genesis, Exodus, Leviticus, Numbers, and Deuteronomy. In keeping with ancient Jewish conventions, the New Testament calls these books "the law of Moses" (Luke 2:22; 24:44; John 7:22; etc.).

As anyone familiar with the Bible knows, the books of the "law" contain more than rules and regulations. In their pages we find many of the most celebrated stories in Scripture, including:

- God's creation of the world and the fall of humanity (Genesis 1–3)

- The narratives about Noah and the Flood (Genesis 6–9)
- God's dealings with Abraham and the other patriarchs (Genesis 12–50)
- The deliverance of Israel from Egypt under Moses (Exodus 1–15)
- Israel's wilderness experience (cf. especially, Exodus 16–40 and the book of Numbers)

In short, for ancient Israel, the "law" was not solely a catalogue of commandments and sanctions. The "law" or the "Torah" referred to biblical narratives of God's dealings with humanity. The individual commandments were inseparably bound up with this story.

### The Law and the Covenant

Within Scripture, God's law is closely aligned with another important concept: the covenant. For ancient Jews, God's law and his covenant were seen as inseparably united. The book of Sirach underscores this connection when it refers to "the law" as "the book of the covenant of the Most High God" (Sirach 24:23). As New Testament scholar John Barclay explains, it would be "unnatural" for ancient Jews to think of God's law apart from the notion of his covenant.[1] The covenant defined God's relationship with his people.

But what is a covenant? In the ancient world covenants were much more than legally binding contracts. The late Old Testament scholar Frank Moore Cross observed that covenants were seen as bringing two parties together as *family*.[2] As one

---

1    Barclay, *Paul and the Gift*, 401.
2    Frank Moore Cross, "Kinship and Covenant in Ancient Israel," in *From Epic to Canon* (Baltimore: Johns Hopkins University Press, 1998), 3–21. See also Scott W. Hahn, *Kinship by Covenant*, Anchor Yale Bible Reference Library (New Haven: Yale University Press, 2009).

in-depth study of ancient covenants concludes: ". . . a covenant implies an adoption into the household, an extension of kinship, the making of a brother."[3]

It is important to stress that covenants were not only made between two individuals. National treaties were also viewed as covenant documents. When nations entered into such alliances with one another, the king of the more powerful nation was identified as "father" by the other, and kings of equal status were spoken of as "brothers."

Moreover, as Jewish scholar Jon D. Levenson has observed, in ancient covenant-treaties the parties agreed to commit themselves to something more than just being family—they had to "love" one another. In this, love was not understood merely as an emotion. "Love" referred to a firm and unwavering commitment to remain faithful and loyal.[4] In a covenant the two parties pledge themselves to one another. One covenant scholar puts it this way: "The idea, 'I am yours, you are mine' underlines every covenant declaration . . . covenant is relational."[5] Covenants, therefore, involve "interpersonal communion," or the gift of self.

This can help us better understand the dynamic between God and Israel in the Old Testament. Scholars have long shown that the book of Deuteronomy broadly follows the structure of treaty-covenants made between nations. Deuteronomy, therefore, presents Israel as a nation that has entered into a covenant alliance with a greater king, namely, the Creator God.

But, of course, the covenant signifies something more than merely God's kingship over Israel. As Deuteronomy underscores, God is Israel's "father" (cf. Deuteronomy 32:6; cf. 1:31; 8:5; 14:1). By virtue of the covenant, Israel is God's *family*. God therefore pledges his *love* to the people.

---

3    Paul Kalluveettil, *Declaration and Covenant* (Rome: Biblical Institute Press, 1982), 205.

4    Jon D. Levenson, *The Love of God: Divine Gift, Human Gratitude, and Mutual Faithfulness in Judaism* (Princeton: Princeton University Press, 2016).

5    Kalluveettil, *Declaration*, 212.

For example, we read, "the LORD set his love upon you and chose you" (Deuteronomy 7:7). In turn, Israel is to love God back. This is seen in the passage Jesus identifies as the "great commandment," the *Shema:* ". . . you shall love the LORD your God with all your heart, and with all your soul, and with all your might" (Deuteronomy 6:5; cf. Matthew 22:37–38).

God's "law," then, did not simply refer to specific commandments. The word also related to the broader story of the Lord's covenant relationship with Israel. Indeed, in the Bible, God's commandments are *always* given within the setting of this larger narrative.

Moreover, through the covenant, God is not merely Israel's judge, king, or lawgiver—God is Israel's father. God's law, therefore, is not simply an expression of his power. The law is ultimately an expression of divine love.

## FULFILLING THE LAW

According to various biblical authors, one does not simply follow the law of the Lord to avoid being punished. Obeying the law leads to happiness. This is because God, the Creator, knows what is best for humanity. The law given to Israel reflects that divine wisdom. Keeping the commandments is therefore the path to human fulfillment.

### God's Law as Wisdom

In the Bible, God's commandments are not viewed as reflecting the arbitrary tastes of the Lord. God's law is given for humanity's own good. In other words, murder is not wrong merely because God finds it distasteful. The Lord abhors murder because it is inherently bad for *us.* Christian tradition has always insisted that all of God's commandments are expressions of divine wisdom and demonstrate concern for humanity.

Psalm 119, the longest of the psalms, celebrates God's law, emphasizing that it imparts "wisdom" and "understanding":

> *Thy commandment makes me wiser* than my enemies,
>     for it is ever with me . . .
> *I understand* more than the aged,
>     for I keep thy precepts . . .
> Through thy precepts I get *understanding*;
>     therefore I hate every false way. (Psalm 119:98, 100, 104)

To follow God's law is to learn what it means to live rightly.

The Lord's commandments thus make true human flourishing possible. God's law leads to life. The psalmist writes: "I will never forget thy precepts; for by them thou hast given me life" (Psalm 119:93). The law is therefore an expression of his love: "Deal with thy servant according to thy steadfast love, and teach me thy statutes" (Psalm 119:124).

The connection between the divine law and life is attested in other biblical books. Baruch speaks of God's "commandments of life" (Baruch 3:9). In addition, Sirach speaks of the Torah as the "law of life" (Sirach 17:11). Sin is the reverse of this—it leads to dissatisfaction, sadness, and death. Instead of promoting communion, sin involves preferring *oneself* to others; it leads to isolation.

Sin also involves self-destructive behavior. Books of the Bible like Proverbs, Sirach, and the Wisdom of Solomon make the point that while sinners may revel in the pleasure of their illicit behavior, such enjoyment is fleeting. As Sirach puts it, "Flee from sin as from a snake; for if you approach sin, it will bite you. . . . The way of sinners is smoothly paved with stones, but at its end is the pit of Hades" (Sirach 21:2, 10).

Disobedience to the divine commandments constitutes a refusal to learn from God's fatherly wisdom. In foolishness, we often think disobedience will bring us happiness. Although it may bring momentary enjoyment, the Lord knows that it will ultimately lead to our destruction. In sum, the Bible teaches that God's law does not stand in the way of our happiness—it seeks to make it possible.

### *The Law as a Disciplinarian*

The New Testament reveals that Christ himself fulfills the law. In the Gospel according to Matthew, Jesus explains, "Think not that I have come to abolish the law and the prophets; I have come not to abolish them but to fulfil them" (Matthew 5:17). He insists that "not an iota, not a dot, will pass from the law until all is accomplished" (Matthew 5:18).

This does not necessarily mean that every directive found in the Old Testament still has binding authority on those in the new covenant. Jesus, for example, insists that divorce and remarriage—a practice explicitly sanctioned in the law of Moses—must be set aside (cf. Mark 10:2–9; Matthew 19:3–12). Why was it permitted in the Old Testament? Jesus explains, "For your hardness of hearts Moses allowed you to divorce your wives, but from the beginning it was not so" (cf. Matthew 19:8). In other words, the law permitted a practice that was not originally part of God's plan because of Israel's sinfulness.

For many of the early Church fathers, Jesus's teaching about divorce and remarriage could be applied to other Old Testament regulations, such as the laws mandating regular animal sacrifice.[6] The early Christian writers pointed out that when the Lord delivered Israel from Egypt, God did not mandate daily bloody sacrifices. Aside from the Passover (Exodus 12–13) and the covenant-making offerings required at Mount Sinai (Exodus 24), God had not yet given an elaborate ritual code to Israel detailing the need for daily animal sacrifices. Justin Martyr and Irenaeus found support

---

6   See Michael Patrick Barber, "'The Yoke of Servitude': Christian Non-Observance of the Law's Cultic Precepts in Patristic Sources," *Letter & Spirit* 7 (2011): 67–90, which traces this interpretation out in various fathers and doctors.

for this view in the book of Jeremiah, where God states: "For in the day that I brought them out of the land of Egypt, *I did not speak to your fathers or command them concerning burnt offerings and sacrifices*" (Jeremiah 7:22).

As doctors of the Church like Augustine and Aquinas observed, it was only after Israel worshipped a golden calf that daily animal sacrifice was imposed upon Israel. Why? They argued the sacrificial laws were an expression of God's fatherly wisdom: the Lord wanted to teach the people of Israel that cattle, sheep, and goats—the gods worshipped by the Egyptians—were not true gods. To teach them this lesson, God compelled the Israelites to slaughter them and offer them as sacrifices to the one true God day in and day out. Ultimately, God wanted to teach them to love *him* above all other gods. These gods would let Israel down; the Lord would not.

This outlook can be rooted in the teaching of the Apostle Paul. In Galatians, he explains that the Law was a "custodian" until the coming of Christ.

> . . . the law was our custodian until Christ came . . . But now that faith has come, we are no longer under a custodian; for in Christ Jesus you are all sons of God, through faith. (Galatians 3:24–26)

The term translated "custodian" (Greek *paidagōgos*) refers to ancient Greco-Roman child-rearing practices. Well-to-do parents would often entrust their children to slaves who had the responsibility of accompanying them to school, disciplining them, protecting them, and teaching them proper manners. When the children reached maturity, they were released from the custodian's authority and enjoyed full status as sons and daughters in the household.

For Paul, the old covenant law had the role of a custodian. When the time of full maturity came—the age of the new covenant, ushered in by Christ—the custodian's job was complete. Paul can therefore say, ". . . we are no longer under a custodian." In Christ, all that the law intended to teach is fulfilled.

### Love Fulfills the Law

According to Paul, the law was ultimately ordered to guide us to love. He writes, ". . . love is the fulfilling of the law" (Romans 13:10). This is specifically fulfilled in Christ, whom Paul calls the "end of the law" (Romans 10:4)—or, as the Greek might be better translated, "the *goal* of the law." Christ fulfills the law by offering himself in love for us.

Jesus will go on in the Gospel according Matthew to explain that the two greatest commandments consist in learning *love*. When asked what the greatest command is, Jesus draws together two passages from the Old Testament:

> "You shall love the Lord your God with all your heart, and with all your soul, and with all your mind" [Deuteronomy 6:5]. This is the great and first commandment. And a second is like it, "You shall love your neighbor as yourself" [Leviticus 19:18]. *On these two commandments depend all the law and the prophets.* (Matthew 22:37–40)

All the commandments are, then, ordered towards imparting one thing: love. Above all else, one must love God. Yet one demonstrates this by loving one's neighbor. Jesus's answer is in essential agreement with Paul's teaching: love fulfills the law.

## SALVATION AS KNOWING THE LORD

### The Divine Life of Love

The New Testament affirms an idea we have already found in the Old Testament—God's commandments lead to life. For example, in the Gospel according to Matthew, Jesus affirms, "If you would enter into life, keep the commandments" (Matthew 19:17). For the New Testament authors, however, this "life" we are called to enter into is more than mere biological life. It is not simply having a pulse. True "life" is found in sharing in divine love.

This lesson is especially emphasized in 1 John. There we read:

> We know that we have passed out of death into life, because we love the brethren. *He who does not love abides in death.* Anyone who hates his brother is a murderer, and you know that no murderer has eternal life abiding in him. *By this we know love, that [Christ] laid down his life for us;* and *we ought to lay down our lives for the brethren.* (1 John 3:14–16)

According to 1 John, to pass from death to life is to learn *love.* In fact, to refuse to love is nothing less than "death." Moreover, true love, we are told, is revealed in Christ, who laid down his own life for our sake. In this, Jesus gives us an example—we are to lay down our lives for others in imitation of him. Love is life, and life is found in giving one's life away. In sum, we pass from death to life by learning to love as Christ loves.

This is precisely the point Jesus makes in the Fourth Gospel. At his Last Supper, Jesus says, "A new commandment I give to you, that you love one another; even as I have loved you, that you also love one another" (John 13:34). How is the commandment to love one another "new"? Was not loving one's neighbor a commandment from the Old Testament?

The reason Jesus's commandment is "new" is because he calls us to a new standard of love: we must love *as he loves,* as he says, "even as I have loved you." Of course, he demonstrates what that love looks like on the cross—it is complete, self-giving love.

What is more, Jesus explains that he wants believers to enter into the very life of love he shares with his Father. Salvation consists in something much more than escaping the fires of damnation. It involves nothing less than entering into the life of love between the Father and the Son. Jesus, speaking of his resurrection, announces, "In that day you will know that I am in my Father, and you in me, and I in you" (John 14:20). 1 John tells us, ". . . our *communion* [Greek *koinonia*] is with the Father and with his Son Jesus Christ" (1 John 1:3).[7] Jesus even says, "As the Father has loved me, so have I loved you" (John 15:9). This is a striking passage—the love the Father has for the Son is given to *us* in Christ.

Furthermore, the divine gift of love given to believers is revealed to be a *personal* gift—the gift *is* a person. Jesus reveals "another Paraclete [Greek *parakletos*]" or "another Counselor," the Spirit whom the Father and Son will send (John 14:16; 16:7). By speaking of "another Paraclete" Jesus refers to the fact that he himself is also a Paraclete (cf. 1 John 2:1). As doctors of the Church such as Thomas Aquinas point out, in all of this we learn that the Spirit is a divine person like Christ.

Salvation consists in sharing in the life of these three persons. It is important to stress that according to Jesus this life is not simply something we enter into in the future. This sharing in the life of the Triune God occurs even in this life. Jesus explains that the Father and the Son will dwell with the believer even in this life: ". . . *we will come to him and make our home with him*" (John 14:23). Likewise, the Spirit is with believers: ". . . the Spirit of truth . . . *dwells with you, and will be in you*" (John 14:17). In sum, we do not need to "go to heaven" to be with the Lord. We already enter into that in this life through Christ.

---

7    RSV-CE adapted. Throughout this book I have changed the RSV's rendering of *koinonia* from "fellowship" to "communion."

### Knowing the Lord

Jesus explains that he himself is the way into life. In particular, he describes himself as the "door of the sheep" (John 10:8). He explains, "I am the door; if any one enters by me, he will be *saved*, and will go in and out and find pasture" (John 10:9). Salvation is found through Christ.

In the next verse, Jesus declares, "I came that they may have life, and have it abundantly" (John 10:10). To enter through Christ is to enter into true life, that is, the Triune God's eternal life of love. Later in the Gospel, Jesus elaborates: "I am the way, and the truth, and the life; no one comes to the Father, but by me" (John 14:6).

Jesus goes on then to describe himself as not only a door, but as the good shepherd. He says, "I am the good shepherd. The good shepherd lays down his life for the sheep . . . I know my own and my own know me, as the Father knows me and I know the Father" (John 10:11, 14). Jesus shows us the way to eternal life by modeling life-giving love. But this love is ordered towards him and his sheep "knowing" one another.

In the Bible, the concept of "knowing" is often used to describe a close personal relationship. In the book of Amos, Israel's unique relationship with the Lord is described in terms of "knowing" God. The Lord explains, "*You only have I known* of all the families of the earth" (Amos 3:2). Deuteronomy also highlights Moses's intimacy with God by saying, ". . . there has not arisen a prophet since in Israel like Moses, *whom the* LORD *knew* face to face" (Deuteronomy 34:10). Likewise, when the Lord commissions Jeremiah as a prophet, God tells him, "Before I formed you in the womb I *knew* you, and before you were born I consecrated you" (Jeremiah 1:5).

Yet look again at what Jesus says: "I *know* my own and my own *know* me, as the Father *knows* me and I *know* the Father" (John 10:14). This passage is breathtaking in its implications. Jesus explains that he knows those who belong to him *as God the Father knows him and he knows the Father.* In other words, the life of abundance Jesus is talking about involves nothing less than participating in the life of love the Father and Son share eternally.

Salvation is not merely following rules. It is not simply a matter of memorizing do's and don'ts of the Bible and observing them. God couches his plan of salvation in covenant language, which, as we have seen, is the language of love and self-gift. God is not merely lawgiver or judge. His commandments are not imposed on us at a whim. God is Father. He gives us laws to lead us to happiness, which is found in his love.

But this raises a question. If salvation is a gift and consists in learning love, why the cross? If God wanted to forgive us, why not just do that? Why does the New Testament speak of Christ's death in terms of his paying the "price" for sin? It is to these questions we now turn. In the next chapter we will consider the deeper meaning of the cross.

## 3

# Not without Cost

You are not your own; *you were bought with a price.*
—1 Corinthians 6:19–20

God has revealed his innermost secret: God himself
is an eternal exchange of love, Father, Son, and Holy
Spirit, and he has destined us to share in that exchange.
—*Catechism of the Catholic Church* §221

In my youth, I was an altar boy. My two favorite responsibilities
were ringing the bells and carrying the cross in the procession
into the church at the beginning of the Mass. In my parish,
there were two options: a metal one, which depicted the Risen
Lord—Jesus's arms were outstretched instead of being nailed
to the cross—and a traditional wooden crucifix.

One day, the wooden crucifix disappeared from the sacristy.
I overheard someone ask about its whereabouts. The priest
responded by saying something about the Risen Lord being
more comforting to people than an image of Jesus dead on the
cross. As we processed into church, I glanced up and saw the
most prominent image in the sanctuary: an enormous, larger-
than-life crucifix. I recall thinking to myself that if the sight
of the smaller processional crucifix caused people difficulties,
using the resurrection cross was not going to help them much.

It was impossible to avoid looking at an image of Jesus's death in our church.

Despite its uncomfortable imagery, there is no way to avoid the message of the cross in the New Testament. The biblical writers explicitly link the cross to our "redemption," a term that for ancient Jews came from the world of economics. St. Paul draws this meaning out more explicitly when he says, "You were bought with a price" (1 Corinthians 6:20).

Popular Catholic devotions use this sort of language frequently. For example, each year when we prepare for Christmas, we typically sing "O Come, O Come, Emmanuel," a hymn in which we petition the Lord to "*ransom* captive Israel."

But why is Jesus's death spoken of as "purchasing" salvation? And if God's grace is "free," why the cross? Could God not forgive us without it? Here we come to a central mystery that stands at the heart of salvation history, namely, the mystery of God's love.[1]

## REDEMPTION AND THE DEBT OF SIN

The New Testament speaks of Christ not only as the "Savior" but also as the "Redeemer." But what does "redemption" mean? For many, the word is simply a synonym for "salvation." Yet this is not entirely correct. In fact, salvation is a broad term which refers to deliverance or rescue. "Redemption" is narrower in meaning than "salvation." It offers an important metaphor to describe *how* one is saved. Specifically, "redemption" is a term taken from the world of economics.

---

1   My discussion of the cross relies heavily on the fuller treatment in Pitre, Barber, and Kincaid, *Paul*, chapter 4.

### Redemption, Economics, and the Family

Already in the Old Testament, God describes his saving work in terms of "redemption." When the Lord speaks to Moses about delivering Israel from slavery to Pharaoh in Egypt, God describes this as "redeeming" the people: ". . . I will deliver you from their bondage, and I will *redeem* you with an outstretched arm" (Exodus 6:6). God is thus frequently spoken of as Israel's "redeemer."

In the Old Testament, the Hebrew word translated "redeemer" is *gōʾēl*. The term is not merely a theological concept. "Redemption" was part of everyday life. It was a concept specifically related to financial imagery, in particular, debt. Indeed, in the ancient world, debt represented a very serious matter.

In the case of an especially grave debt, a person could sell off one's ancestral land to pay off a creditor (Leviticus 25:25–34). This represented a drastic course of action. In agrarian societies like ancient Israel's, the land was a family's principal source of income. If even selling off your land would not suffice to pay off the debt, you might be forced to sell yourself into slavery (cf. Leviticus 25:39, 47–48). This meant catastrophic personal ruin. In some cases, your spouse and children could also apparently be taken as slaves (cf. 2 Kings 4:1–7).

Nonetheless, the destitute still had hope. According to biblical law, a "redeemer" (*gōʾēl*) could "buy back" another person's land and/or freedom. This task fell to a family member: ". . . *one of his* [the debtor's] *brothers may redeem him*, or *his uncle*, or *his cousin may redeem him*, or *a near kinsman belonging to his family may redeem him*" (cf. Leviticus 25:48–49). The point to underscore here is this: redemption was primarily *a family affair*.

This sheds important light on the biblical story. In Exodus 6, when God promises to deliver his people, he ties this to his *covenant* promises to Israel's forefathers, Abraham, Isaac, and Jacob, explaining, "I also established my covenant with them" (Exodus 6:4). God says he will "redeem" Israel because "I have remembered my covenant" (Exodus 6:5). By taking on the role of Israel's "redeemer," the Lord is shown to be family to Israel. As we have seen, by virtue of the covenant, God and Israel are united in a familial bond. Redemption is a *family* matter.

### Sin, Redemption, and the New Covenant

As we have seen, "redemption" is an economic concept. In connection with this, it is significant to note that in ancient Judaism sin was understood as a "debt." Jesus alludes to this traditional Jewish view when he gives the disciples the words of the "Our Father." Specifically, he tells them to pray, ". . . forgive us our *debts*, as we also have forgiven our *debtors*" (Matthew 6:12).

The language is especially appropriate within a covenant relationship. As we have mentioned, the Jewish scholar Jon D. Levenson notes that a covenant was understood to be a bond of love. In a way, the two parties can be thought of as *owing* love to one another. Sin is a debt within the logic of a relationship defined by *love*. God thus frequently refers to his *love* for Israel as an expression of his faithfulness to the covenant.

In the New Testament, Jesus's death is specifically linked not only to God's love but to covenant imagery. At the Last Supper, Jesus takes the cup and says, "This cup which is poured out for you is *the new covenant* in my blood" (Luke 22:20; cf. 1 Corinthians 11:25). With these words, Jesus alludes to one of the most important prophecies in the Old Testament, which is found in the book of Jeremiah.

In Jeremiah 31, God announces his plan to save his people. This plan is rooted in divine love: "I have loved you with an everlasting love; therefore I have continued my faithfulness to you" (Jeremiah 31:3). Going on, God tells Israel to rejoice because, "The LORD has *saved* his people, the remnant of Israel" (Jeremiah 31:7). This salvation is then described in terms of "redemption" and "ransom": ". . . the LORD has *ransomed* Jacob, and has *redeemed* him from hands too strong for him" (Jeremiah 31:11). As in the Exodus, God promises to once again take up the role as the people's Redeemer. In doing so, the Lord expresses covenant faithfulness and acts as family to Israel.

Not surprisingly, as in Exodus, God's promise of redemption is linked to the *covenant*. This time God speaks of establishing a "new covenant," through which Israel would *know* the Lord and sins would be forgiven. Although lengthy, it is worth reading the words of the Lord's promise carefully.

> I will make *a new covenant* with the house of Israel and the house of Judah, not like the covenant which I made with their fathers when I took them by the hand to bring them out of the land of Egypt, *my covenant which they broke.* But this is the covenant which I will make with the house of Israel after those days, says the LORD: I will put my law within them, and I will write it upon their hearts . . . And no longer shall each man teach his neighbor and each his brother, saying, "Know the LORD," for they shall all know me, from the least of them to the greatest, says the LORD; *for I will forgive their iniquity, and I will remember their sin no more.*" (Jeremiah 31:31–33, 34)

This prophecy will have important significance not only for our discussion here but for later chapters in this book as well.

For now, let me highlight one key feature of the prophet's announcement—we are told *why* a new covenant is necessary, namely, the former covenant had been broken because of sin. Here Jeremiah is referring to the events in the book of Exodus. We now turn to consider the story of that first covenant in greater detail.

## REDEMPTION AND ATONEMENT

The story of how God's covenant with Israel was not only established but also broken is found in the book of Exodus. At the center of the narrative is Moses. When Israel sins, Moses tells the people that he will go to the Lord and ask for forgiveness on their behalf. In particular, Moses uses an important word: "atonement." As we shall see, this word has important meaning for understanding how Christ's work of redemption is ultimately a revelation of God's love.

### *Covenant Blood-Guilt*

We have already seen that the covenant is a key concept in Scripture. Jeremiah even speaks of God's covenant with the day and the night (Jeremiah 33:25), language that suggests the notion that God had forged a covenant with creation itself. In Jeremiah 31, however, the focus is on God's covenant relationship with Israel.

Most people with passing familiarity with the Bible know that it describes Israel as God's "covenant people." The crucial account of how that bond was established is found in the book of Exodus. There we learn that the covenant between God and Israel was ratified through a sacrificial ceremony that involved highly symbolic imagery. To our modern ears, the details of this ceremony appear strange and morbid. Yet the rituals it involved were rich in symbolic meaning. As we shall see, they also shed light on the New Testament's teaching on the meaning of Christ's death.

Moses directs young men to slay sacrificial animals. Once the animals are slaughtered, Moses ratifies the covenant through an elaborate ritual involving the sacrificial victims' blood:

> Moses took half of the blood and put it in basins, and half of the blood he threw against the altar. Then he took the book of

the covenant, and read it in the hearing of the people; and they said, "All that the LORD has spoken we will do, and we will be obedient." And Moses took the blood and threw it upon the people, and said, "Behold the blood of the covenant which the LORD has made with you in accordance with all these words." (Exodus 24:6–8)

What is the meaning of all of this?

Moses's actions are tightly bound up with the logic of ancient covenant-making. For one thing, by putting blood on both the altar—which represents God—and on the people, Moses signifies that God and the people now share a "blood bond." In other words, the covenant makes God and the people family.

Furthermore, note that Moses only puts the blood on the people *after* they reiterate their commitment to keep the covenant: "All that the LORD has spoken, we will do." With this we come to a crucial point: in biblical times, covenant-making was closely related to *oath swearing*. This is evident, for example, in Psalm 89, where God says, "I have made a covenant with my chosen one, I have sworn to David my servant" (Psalms 89:3). Here as in other places in Scripture, covenant and oath are nearly interchangeable terms (cf. Psalms 105:9). When the people promise obedience, they are swearing an oath of covenant fidelity.

Why was oath-swearing such an essential element of establishing a covenant? By swearing an oath, one appealed to a divine witness who was understood as enforcing the covenant's terms. The divine witness would ensure that those who were faithful to their sworn oath would be blessed and those who were not would be cursed.

All of this was expressed by sacrifice. The ritual death of the animal was a kind of "self-curse." The sacrifice symbolized the fate of those who transgressed their oath. As later Jewish interpreters recognized, this is one of the reasons Moses sprinkles the blood of the offerings on the people. One ancient rabbi summed up the meaning of the symbolism this way:

> When a king administers an oath to his legions, he does so with a sword, the implication being: Whoever transgresses these conditions, let the sword pass over his neck. Similarly [at Sinai], *Moses took half of the blood . . .*"[2]

In short, by killing the animals at Sinai, the Israelites ritually acted out the covenant curse that would befall them if they failed to remain faithful. Unfortunately, as Jeremiah's oracle observes, that is precisely what Israel did.

### Atonement as Ransom

After reading about how the Israelites entered into a covenant with God, we go on to read in Exodus about how they broke it by worshipping an idol, a golden calf (cf. Exodus 32). When Moses learns of this, he smashes the tablets of the Ten Commandments (Exodus 32:19), symbolizing the fact that the covenant had been broken. By violating their oath, Israel had triggered the covenant curse of death.

Recognizing the gravity of the situation, Moses tells the people that he will attempt to intercede on their behalf to God. Here we encounter terminology used in the New Testament to describe Jesus's salvific work: atonement. Moses says, "I will go up to the LORD; perhaps I can *make atonement for your sin*" (Exodus 32:30). In context, the meaning of "atonement" is clear: Moses seeks to somehow save Israel from the deadly consequences of breaking the covenant.

---

2   *Midrash Rabbah Leviticus 6.6*; Harry Freedman and Maurice Simon, eds., *Midrash Rabbah Leviticus* (London: The Soncino Press, 1983), 83. Though this is a much later text it captures more ancient attitudes regarding covenant-making (cf. Jeremiah 34:18).

Moses then goes up Mount Sinai and asks the Lord to "forgive" (Hebrew *nāśāʾ*) the people (Exodus 32:30–34). In essence, Moses beseeches God "not to execute the penalty which their sin deserved."[3] Atonement and forgiveness are here interrelated. This raises the question: what does "atonement" mean?

Among other things, the word "atonement" (Hebrew *kipper*) can have the sense of "ransom." This can be seen in the Torah's regulations for dealing with a murderer. We read:

> . . . you shall accept no *ransom for the life* of a murderer, who is guilty of death; but *he shall be put to death*. And you shall accept no *ransom* for him who has fled . . . for blood pollutes the land, and no *atonement* can be made for the land, for the blood that is shed in it, except by the blood of him who shed it." (Numbers 35:31–33)[4]

In this passage, "atonement" refers to delivering a person from death by means of a payment, that is, a "ransom."

In the Old Testament, some sacrifices, such as those associated with the Day of Atonement, seem to serve as a "ransom." Interestingly, by the first century AD, the Jubilee Year, which was proclaimed on the Day of Atonement (Leviticus 25:8–10), was connected to the forgiveness of debts. It is no surprise then that the Dead Scrolls describe the day of future redemption in terms of a Jubilee Year in which Israel's debt of sin is forgiven.

In Exodus, Moses seeks to atone for Israel's sins. God later gives Israel various sacrifices through which atonement can be made. The New Testament reveals that these offerings anticipated and foreshadowed Christ's self-offering (cf. Hebrews 8:5). Jesus pays the price of sin by making an offering

---

3    Jay Sklar, *Sin, Impurity, Sacrifice, and Atonement* (Sheffield: Sheffield Phoenix Press, 2005), 92.
4    RSV-CE slightly adapted for consistency.

of himself by pouring out his blood, which he calls the "blood of the covenant" (Matthew 26:28).

### Christ's Atoning Death and God's Love

Our examination of the Old Testament background for the New Testament's teaching brings the meaning of various texts we find into sharper focus. In Colossians we read that Jesus's death dissolves the "debt" humanity owed to God: "[God] has forgiven us all our trespasses, by *canceling the record of debt* that stood against us with its legal demands. This he set aside, nailing it to the cross" (Colossians 2:13–14).[5]

Sin is a debt. Christ pays the price of "redemption" to save us from it by giving his very self on our behalf. As Jesus says in the Gospels of Matthew, he came to "give his life as a *ransom* for many" (Matthew 20:28; Mark 10:45; cf. also Ephesians 1:7; 1 Peter 1:18–19). The imagery is metaphorical and should not be pressed too far. Still, the New Testament uses it to help us understand aspects of Christ's work—Jesus not only frees us from the debt of sin but also its consequences: slavery to sin (Romans 6:6–7).

In other places, "atonement" language is used. Paul speaks of the "*redemption* that is in Christ Jesus, whom God put forward as *a sacrifice of atonement by his blood*" (Romans 3:24–25).[6] Even more explicit is the letter to the Hebrews, which goes into detail in connecting Jesus's death to the imagery of the Day of Atonement. The point is this: Christ makes atonement possible by his sacrificial love.

Moreover, Paul highlights the covenantal dimension of Christ's death. In Galatians 3, Paul reminds his readers that all who are under the law are bound to keep it. Failure to do so, he reminds his audience, triggers the covenant curse (Galatians 3:10). Yet God's people did not keep the

---

5    English Standard Version.
6    English Standard Version.

covenant. Christ, therefore, comes to bring "redemption" from that curse: "Christ has *redeemed* us from the curse of the law by becoming a curse for us" (Galatians 3:13).[7] The Apostle explains that because Jesus bore the curse of death redemptively, God's promises to Abraham to bless all nations can finally be realized.

In other words, Christ's death brings about the fulfillment of God's plan. The Lord had promised Abraham that all nations would be blessed through his line (cf. Genesis 22:18). Yet by sinning and placing themselves under the curse of the covenant, his descendants, the Israelites, put the promised blessing on hold. By dying on the cross, Christ unleashes the blessing upon all.

In all of this, the message of the New Testament underscores the notion emphasized by Jeremiah—God saves his people out of *love*. Jesus was not coerced into dying on the cross. The biblical writers insist that Jesus gave himself *freely*. The cross was not "necessary" because God was somehow painted into a corner by humanity's sinfulness. The Father was not forced to deliver up the Son because earlier promises could not be broken. On the contrary, God acts freely. The promises were made by God who already knew what they would entail.

God's plan all along was to answer our sinfulness with an act of love. Paul, for example, indicates that the cross is foreshadowed in the story of Abraham, who was called upon to offer his only beloved son, Isaac, as a sacrifice in Genesis 22. In Romans 8:32, the Apostle says God "did not spare [Greek *epheisato*]" Jesus, using language that parallels the story of Abraham's fidelity. In this Paul suggests that even in Genesis God knew *precisely* how salvation history would play out. He anticipated humanity's sin and planned to use its consequences for his purposes. This brings us to the deepest truth about the cross: it is a revelation of God's love.

---

7   New Revised Standard Version Catholic Edition.

## THE CROSS AS THE REVELATION OF DIVINE LOVE

Why the cross? By laying down his life, Jesus revealed the most profound truth about who God is: God is love. In this we find the central truth of the mystery of our salvation.

### *Divine Love and the Cross*

Paul offers a particularly profound reflection on the nature of the cross in Philippians 2. Using words many believe he borrowed from a well-known early Christian hymn or poem, Paul writes:

> Have this mind among yourselves, which was in Christ Jesus, who, though he was in the form of God, did not count equality with God a thing to be grasped, but emptied himself, taking the form of a servant, being born in the likeness of men. And being found in human form he humbled himself and became obedient unto death, even death on a cross. Therefore God has highly exalted him and bestowed on him the name which is above every name, that at the name of Jesus every knee should bow, in heaven and on earth and under the earth, and every tongue confess that Jesus Christ is Lord, to the glory of God the Father. (Philippians 2:5–11).

Three important features of this passage are worth highlighting.[8]

First, in these verses Paul uses language that Christian tradition has long understood as describing the incarnation: Jesus was first in the "form of God" and then went on to take the "form of a servant," being "born in the likeness of men." Since taking the "form of a servant" means becoming human, when Paul speaks of Jesus being in the "form of God," he therefore must mean something similar. The passage even tells us what being in the "form of God" means. It entails "equality with God." In fact, Paul elsewhere describes Jesus as the one

---

8    The explanation of this passage that follows is a summary of the exegetical analysis found in Pitre, Barber, and Kincaid, *Paul*, chapter 3.

Lord of Israel, the God identified in Deuteronomy 6:4 (cf. 1 Corinthians 8:6). In sum, Philippians 2 affirms that Jesus was a divine person who became man.

Second, Paul maintains that Jesus *freely* humbled himself. The Apostle insists that Jesus did not consider "equality with God" a thing to be "grasped." As commentators have pointed out, the Greek word that is translated "grasped" (Greek *harpagmos*) has the connotation of "a thing to be exploited." In other words, what Paul appears to be saying is that Jesus did not cling to his divinity in order to exploit it for himself. Paul never suggests that Jesus stopped being God. His point is that Jesus freely chose to humble himself by taking on a human nature. As a man, he was "obedient," submitting his human will to the divine will. The cross is the ultimate expression of this obedience.

Third and most poignantly, the passage describes Jesus's descent as involving two stages. First, as God, Jesus empties himself in taking the nature of a servant—i.e., in becoming human. Second, as man, Jesus empties himself in a further way by embracing the humiliation of death on a cross. This is a profound dimension of the passage that bears careful reflection.

What Jesus does on the cross in the "form of a servant" is an expression of what it means for him to be "in the form of God." By accepting death on the cross, Jesus is not acting in a way that contradicts his divinity. Rather, his faithfulness unto death is expressive of it. *By giving himself freely on the cross, Jesus makes manifest what it means to be God.* For Paul, the cross reveals God's *love.*

### *The Cross as Revelation of Divine Love and Perfect Humanity*
We can now return to our original question: why the cross? First and foremost, the cross is *revelatory.* It shows us what divinity looks like—it is made manifest in self-giving love. Divinity is not just awe-inspiring power. Behind that majesty and might is God's innermost secret: "God is love" (1 John 4:8).

The New Testament writers tell us that the ultimate goal of the divine plan is for God to enter into communion with humanity through Christ. In 1 John we read: ". . . that which we have seen and heard we proclaim also to you, so that you may have *communion* (Greek *koinōnian*) with us; and *our communion* (Greek *koinōnian*) *is with the Father and with his Son Jesus Christ*" (1 John 1:3). Another important passage is found in 2 Peter 1:4, which insists that God's plan is ultimately ordered to make humanity *"partakers of the divine nature."* Many other similar passages could be mentioned.

Salvation is not simply about being forgiven of sin. It is, in the final analysis, about being united to God. Humanity is created for a purpose, namely, to share in the Trinity's own life of love. As Philippians 2 indicates, Christ's act of self-giving reveals what it means to be "in the form of God"—it means total self-donation. This is what God wants humanity to enter into by grace.

### Love as the Cost of Salvation

To be sure, Jesus's death was not strictly *necessary*. God was not obligated to save humanity from sin. God could have saved us in some other way. Yet the cross was the most *fitting way* to save us because it reveals that God is love.

Moreover, Jesus shows us what it means to be "fully human." In dying on the cross, Jesus reveals what this involves—we are called to image God by pouring out our lives in love. Put simply, we were made to love. Love is what fulfills us. Jesus therefore explains, "For whoever would save his life will lose it, and whoever loses his life for my sake will find it" (Matthew 16:25).

In the very passage where we read the famous line "God is love," 1 John spells all of this out in a concise way:

> *Whoever does not love does not know God, for God is love.* God's love was revealed among us in this way: God sent his only Son

into the world so that we might live through him. In this is love, *not that we loved God but that he loved us* and sent his Son *to be the atoning sacrifice for our sins.* Beloved, since God loved us so much, we also ought to love one another. No one has ever seen God; if we love one another, *God lives in us, and his love is perfected in us.* (1 John 4:8–12)[9]

This rich and beautiful text brings together the various ideas we have been considering. First, the deepest truth about the divine life is that it is defined by love. Second, this truth is revealed not only in the incarnation—the sending of the Son—but in Christ's death. Third, Jesus's death is described in terms of "atonement," which addresses the problem of sin. Sin is overcome through the life-giving love of the Son. Finally, the cross is more than a demonstration of God's love; it enables God's love to be perfected in believers who fulfill what it means to share in God's life by learning to love as they have been loved.

The cross is uncomfortable—it bespeaks the consequences of sin and the total self-gift that is demanded of us. To downplay the cross can have dangerous consequences for our spiritual life. To minimize the role of the cross in salvation neglects the true danger of sin. The cross unmasks sin in all of its horror. Sin is sorrow, pain, violence, death, and destruction. In a world that fails to recognize the seriousness of disobedience to God, the cross stands as a sign of contradiction. It exposes the lie that sin is "no big deal." On the cross, we see Jesus take on all of the ghastly consequences of sin.

Yet the death of the divine Son also highlights the wondrous nature of salvation. The cross reminds us that salvation is "free" but not "cheap." The less we reflect on the cross, the less we are likely to consider the depth of God's love for us. St. Thomas Aquinas observed that Paul exhorts the Corinthians

---

9  New Revised Version Catholic Edition.

that they were "bought with a price" (1 Corinthians 6:20) for good reason. By considering the cost of our redemption, Thomas Aquinas says, we are "all the more bound to refrain from sin."[10]

Through the cross, Jeremiah's prophecy is fulfilled—the broken relationship with him due to sin is overcome; his people can truly *know* him (Jeremiah 31:34). Yet salvation involves more than just communion with God in Christ. It also means union with all others who are united to him. We cannot be saved apart from Christ; but we also cannot be saved apart from all others in communion with him as well. Salvation truly is a *family* affair. Contrary to what you may have heard, salvation is *not* simply a "personal relationship with Jesus." It includes others as well. This is the aspect of salvation we consider in our next chapter.

---

10    *Summa Theologiae* III, q. 46, art. 3.

# 4

# Not Just Personal

The bread which we break, is it not a communion in the
body of Christ? Because there is one bread, we who are
many are one body, for we all partake of the one bread.
—1 Corinthians 10:16–17

Sacraments are "powers that comes forth" from the Body
of Christ . . . They are actions of the Holy Spirit at work
in his Body, the Church. They are "the masterworks of
God" in the new and everlasting covenant.
—*Catechism of the Catholic Church* §1116

It had been a long flight but, frankly, it had gone by in a
blur. Since takeoff, I had been reading an excellent book that
examined Jesus's teachings in light of Jewish traditions. As we
began our final descent, I tucked the book back in my bag. It
was at this point that the stranger sitting next to me spoke for
the first time.

"I noticed the cover," he said, nodding towards my bag.
"Are you a Christian?"

"Even better," I said with a smile. "I'm a Catholic."

The stranger looked surprised. "I didn't realize Catholics
were Christians," he responded. He added, "Would you say
you have a personal relationship with Jesus?"

For many people, Christian faith is *merely* about a "personal relationship with Jesus." I suspected I knew where the conversation would go from that point on and I turned out to be correct. I was told that Catholicism is "organized religion." True Christian faith is "really only about one thing—me and Jesus." One cannot have a meaningful relationship with Jesus *and* belong to an institutional Church.

I readily affirm that salvation is about entering into a relationship with the Lord. The *Catechism* rightly describes the mystery of faith as "a vital and *personal relationship* with the living and true God" (§2558).[1] Those who think that viewing faith as a personal relationship necessarily rules out the need for membership in the visible and institutional Church insist on a false choice.

Yet salvation cannot only be about "me and Jesus." As we saw in chapter 2, the New Testament reveals that God is a communion of persons. For the New Testament authors, salvation involves sharing in the inner life of the Triune God. But salvation is not only about communion with the Triune God, it is also about communion with others, namely, those who are also in God in Christ. Paul therefore says that God has called believers "into the *communion* of his Son, Jesus Christ our Lord" (1 Corinthians 1:9). Elsewhere Paul links this idea of communion with Christ's "body," the "Church" (cf. 1 Corinthians 10:16–17).

In this chapter we will look more carefully at the New Testament's teaching about the Church. Of course, our discussion will raise important questions such as whether those "outside the Church" can be saved. Yet before addressing those issues we need to understand what the New Testament says about the nature of the Church itself. As we shall see, the role of the Church in salvation is inextricably linked to an

---

1    Emphasis added.

idea we have already underscored: salvation in Christ truly is a family affair.

## THE CHURCH IN THE NEW TESTAMENT

The New Testament authors use many different images for the Church. Here let us focus on four: body, temple, family, and bride. Though these aspects of the Church's identity may at first seem disconnected, a closer look reveals that they are in fact closely interrelated.

### *The Church as Body*

To explain how believers are united to one another in Christ, Paul uses the image of a body. He writes, ". . . we, though many, are *one body in Christ*, and *individually members one of another*" (Romans 12:5). Because of this spiritual union, what happens to one believer has implications for the whole body: "*If one member suffers, all suffer together; if one member is honored, all rejoice together*" (1 Corinthians 12:26). Paul identifies this body as the "church" (1 Corinthians 12:27–28; cf. Colossians 1:18; Ephesians 1:22; 5:23)

Paul speaks of "churches" in the plural where he refers to the different Christ-believing communities in various locations. For instance, he tells those in Rome, "All the *churches* of Christ greet you" (Romans 16:16). Nevertheless, this should not give the impression that there are different *bodies* of Christ. Paul also uses "church" in the singular. For example, he says, "I persecuted *the church* of God" (1 Corinthians 15:9). All of the different "churches" are part of a single community—there is only *one body*. Paul writes,

> For just as the body is one and has many members, and all the members of the body, though many, are one body, so it is with Christ. For by one Spirit we were all baptized into

> one body—Jews or Greeks, slaves or free—and all were
> made to drink of one Spirit. For the body does not consist
> of one member but of many. (1 Corinthians 12:12–14)

Following this, Catholic teaching recognizes that while there
are distinct "churches," which are primarily distinguished by
geographical location, there is also *one* "Church."

Christ is present in believers, but not in an individualistic
way. This point is emphasized in the book of Acts. There we
read about the event that caused "Saul, the Persecutor of the
Church" to become "Paul, the Apostle of Christ." While
traveling on the road to Damascus, Saul encounters the Risen
Lord, who puts to him a key question: "Saul, *why do you
persecute me?*" (Acts 9:4). Saul, perplexed, asks who is speaking
to him. The life-changing response he receives is, "*I am Jesus,
whom you are persecuting*" (Acts 9:5)

Saul might have responded, "But Lord, I am not persecuting
*you*. I am targeting those who believe in you." Yet that is the
key point—Jesus is united to his Church. What Saul does to
the Church, he does to Christ himself.

For the New Testament, Christ is now acting in the
Church. What he did in his personal body, he now does in
his mystical body. The Church is, as St. Augustine said, the
"whole Christ." As St. Ignatius of Antioch wrote in the early
second century, ". . . where there is Christ Jesus, there is the
catholic church."[2]

### The Church as Temple

This notion of the Church as "body" is closely bound up
with another idea, namely, that it is a "temple." In the Old
Testament, the temple was the place of God's holy presence.
According to the New Testament, God has become man and
walked among us. Jesus is Emmanuel, that is, "God with

---

2   *Letter to the Syrnaeans* 8.2.

us" (Matthew 1:23; cf. 28:20). Naturally, then, the New Testament identifies Jesus as the temple. In John 2, Jesus declares, "*Destroy this temple and in three days I will raise it up*" (John 2:19). While his hearers think he is referring to the Jerusalem temple, we are told, ". . . he spoke of *the temple of his body*" (John 2:21).

Temple imagery is also applied to Jesus in the other Gospels. For example, drawing from Psalm 118:22, Jesus says of himself: "The very stone which the builders rejected has become the head of the corner" (Mark 12:10). In its original context, the psalm is best read as describing a temple-building project (cf. Psalm 118:26–27). That Jesus quotes the psalm while teaching in the temple confirms that an allusion to the holy building is intended (Matthew 24:2; Mark 13:1–2; Luke 21:5–6).

What is particularly noteworthy is that Jesus refers to himself as merely the "cornerstone." By this Jesus indicates that there is more to the temple than just himself. Commentators often recognize that Jesus's saying points to the role of the wider community of believers—the Church. In fact, 1 Peter explicitly draws this point out:

> Come to him, to that living stone, rejected by men but in God's sight chosen and precious; and *like living stones be yourselves built into a spiritual house, to be a holy priesthood, to offer spiritual sacrifices* acceptable to God through Jesus Christ. . . . To you therefore who believe, he is precious, but for those who do not believe, "The very stone which the builders rejected has become the head of the corner." (1 Peter 2:4–5, 7)

The Church is united to Christ and "built into him," forming a temple. Believers are called to be like Christ, offering their sacrifices in union with him.

In 2 Corinthians 6, Paul writes: "For we are the temple of the living God" (2 Corinthians 6:16). The Church's identity as temple is also expressed in Ephesians, where the imagery is connected with two other important images: the Church as the "household" (or "family") of God and the Church as Christ's bride. These merit closer attention.

### The Church as Family and Bride

As we have seen, according to the New Testament, salvation is a family matter. It is no wonder, then, that the Church is specifically identified as the "household" or "family" of God. In Galatians 6:10, Paul speaks of the Church as "the household of faith."

Especially noteworthy is Ephesians 2, which connects the Church's identity as both body and temple with "family" language. First, we read that Christ is the one who came to save both Jews and Gentiles together "*in one body* through the cross" (Ephesians 2:16). We are then told that all believers are

> members of *the household of God*, built upon the foundation of the apostles and prophets, *Christ Jesus himself being the cornerstone*, in whom *the whole structure is joined together* and *grows into a holy temple in the Lord*; *in whom you also are built into it for a dwelling place of God in the Spirit.* (Ephesians 2:19–22)

In this rich passage, the Church is not only portrayed as the "household of God," it is also depicted as a temple. The connection would have seemed natural since the temple was frequently described as God's "house."

Moreover, observe how the metaphors for the Church are merged. Buildings do not usually "grow" and bodies are not "built." The combination of these three images—family, body, and temple—is no accident. The Church is a family because all believers share in Christ's divine sonship, making them all children. Those who are saved are made one in Christ. And since Christ himself is the cornerstone of the true temple, all who are saved in him are built into that same temple-community. Finally, since the Church is a family, the identity of the Church as a temple—a "house"—makes perfect sense.

Yet Ephesians adds another image to describe the Church: the Church as Christ's "bride." This idea is inseparable from its role as Christ's body. We read:

> . . . husbands should love their wives *as their own bodies.* He who loves his *wife loves himself. For no man ever hates his own flesh, but nourishes and cherishes it, as Christ does the church,* because we are members of his body. "For this reason a man shall leave his father and mother and be joined to his wife, and the *two shall become one flesh*" [Genesis 2:24]. *This is a great mystery, and I mean in reference to Christ and the church.* (Ephesians 5:28–32)

We can easily misunderstand the "body of Christ" metaphor used for the Church. The point is *not* that the Church is a headless torso. In marriage, two become so truly united that they become "one flesh," that is, "one body." When a husband loves his wife, he "loves *himself*" and cares for his "*own*" flesh." The Church is the body of Christ because the Church is his bride.

Christ is united to believers, but not in an individualistic way. Christ has *one* bride. All believers are therefore saved together as part of this one body, the bride of Christ.

All of the images we have been looking at, therefore, fit together and should not be seen as disconnected perspectives on the Church. The Church is saved by being united to Christ. Believers are not saved apart from one another, but through being united to the "whole Christ," namely, his body, the Church.[3] This union is covenantal—it is marital and, therefore, familial. Salvation really is a family affair.

---

3    Augustine, *On Christian Doctrine* 3.31.44.

## ONE BREAD, ONE BODY

According to the New Testament authors, salvation is attained by being united with Christ. The letters of Paul teach that this union is realized through Baptism and the Eucharist. For the biblical authors, the sacraments have a crucial role in salvation. Yet they are also about more than initiating a *personal* relationship with Jesus. These sacraments unite the believer to all the members of his body. Salvation is personal, but it is also *communal.*

### Baptized into One Body

According to 1 Peter, salvation occurs through Baptism. We read, "*Baptism . . . now saves you*, not as a removal of dirt from the body but as an appeal to God for a clear conscience, through the resurrection of Jesus Christ" (1 Peter 3:21). Baptism is no mere symbol, but effects *salvation*—it "now saves you."

The New Testament also reports that Peter stressed the importance of Baptism when he spoke to the crowds after the Spirit had descended upon the apostles during the Jewish festival of Pentecost. After hearing Peter proclaim the Gospel message, the people ask the apostles, "Brethren, what shall we do?" Peter responds, "Repent, and be baptized every one of you" (Acts 2:38). The fisherman goes on to speak of being "saved" (Acts 2:40). As in 1 Peter, Peter's speech in Acts links salvation and Baptism.

In addition, Paul writes that it is through Baptism that one shares in the saving effects of Christ's death: "Do you not know that *all of us who have been baptized* into Christ Jesus were *baptized into his death*?" (Romans 6:3). Here Paul does not seem to be introducing a new idea but appears to be reminding them of something they should already have known.

In Galatians 3, Paul maintains,

> . . . for in Christ Jesus you are all *sons of God*, through faith. *For as many of you as were baptized into Christ have put on Christ.* There is neither Jew nor Greek, there is neither slave nor free, there is neither male nor female; for *you are all one in Christ Jesus.* (Galatians 3:26–28)

To be baptized is the equivalent of "putting on Christ." Still, for Paul, Baptism is not only about union with Christ. The Apostle insists, ". . . by one Spirit we *were all baptized into one body*" (1 Corinthians 12:13). Through Baptism, one is united not only to Christ but to the larger household of faith, the family of God, the "one body."

### *Communal Healing*

Through Baptism, which is received at the hands of another, one receives new life in Christ. But one also finds healing through others whom God uses as his instruments. James writes,

> Is any among you sick? Let him call for the elders of the church, and let them pray over him, anointing him with oil in the name of the Lord; and the prayer of faith will save the sick man, and the Lord will raise him up; and if he has committed sins, he will be forgiven. Therefore confess your sins to one another, and pray for one another, that you may be healed. The prayer of a righteous man has great power in its effects. (James 5:14–16)

Healing is not received from Jesus *apart* from others. Christ brings it to us *through* the working of others.

Moreover, the sick are to call for the "elders." In Greek, the word for "elders" is *presbyters* (*presbyteroi*), the word from which we get the English word "priests." These elders are to pray over the sick. When James goes on to say, "confess your sins to one another" and "pray for one another," recall that he has already indicated that the ministers are specifically called upon to carry out the role of praying over the sick. In context, then, the sick person has the elder both pray over him *and* hear his sins.

In this passage we see the roots of the Church's practice of the sacrament of Penance (Confession) and Anointing of the Sick, which express the conviction that Christ's saving work is carried out in and through others.

### Communion with Christ's Body in the Eucharist

Although Paul taught that the Church should be understood as Christ's "body," he himself tells us that Jesus used that same language when he instituted the Eucharist. He reminds the Corinthians of a tradition they already know—Jesus took bread at the Last Supper and, over it, spoke the words, "*This is my body which is for you*" (1 Corinthians 11:24). As others have suggested, Paul's teaching that the Church is Christ's "body" likely originated out of the Apostle's reflection on the Eucharist.[4]

Paul maintains that it is through the Eucharist that one has communion with Christ: "The bread which we break, is it not a *communion* [Greek *koinōnia*] in the body of Christ? Because there is one bread, we who are many are one body, for we all partake of the one bread" (1 Corinthians 10:16–17). The force of Paul's language should not be overlooked. Paul does not believe that the Eucharist merely symbolizes communion with Christ; the Apostle teaches that the Church is Christ's body *because* it shares in the "one bread."

## IS THERE SALVATION OUTSIDE THE CHURCH?

Following the New Testament's teaching that salvation involves being united to the whole body of Christ, the Catholic

---

4    See E. P. Sanders, *Paul: The Apostle's Life, Letters, and Thought* (Minneapolis: Fortress, 2015), 720–21.

Church maintains that salvation cannot simply be construed in individualistic terms. St. Cyprian of Carthage, writing in the third century, insisted, "He can no longer have God for his Father who has not the church for his mother."[5] Later councils and popes would articulate this understanding with an ancient formulation received from Cyprian, namely, that there is "no salvation outside the Church" (Latin *extra ecclesiam nulla salus*).[6] This teaching must be properly understood. It should not be construed as indicating that non-Catholics are necessarily going to hell.

### The Possibility of Salvation for the Unbaptized

The New Testament is clear: Jesus is the *only* way to the Father. In the Gospel according to John, Jesus says, "I am the way, and the truth, and the life; no one comes to the Father, but by me" (John 14:6). Likewise, in the book of Acts, Peter proclaims Jesus is the messiah, by saying, ". . . there is salvation in no one else, for there is no other name under heaven given among men by which we must be saved" (Acts 4:12).

This does not mean that those who do not explicitly confess faith in Jesus cannot be saved. For one thing, the New Testament authors are adamant about the salvation of certain figures *prior* to Christ. For example, there can be little doubt that the New Testament authors thought that the patriarch Abraham was saved. In the Gospel according to John, Jesus says, "Abraham rejoiced that he was to see my day; he saw it and was glad" (John 8:56). In the Gospel of Luke, Jesus even alludes to Abraham's prominent place in the afterlife (Luke 16:19–31). Moreover, in addition to Abraham, Hebrews 11 provides a long list of figures who were examples of faith prior to the coming of Christ.

---

5 Cyprian, *On the Unity of the Church*, 6.
6 See, e.g., Cyprian, *Epistle* 72.21 and the Fourth Lateran Council under Pope Innocent III (1215).

How could figures such as Abraham or Job have faith? If Abraham and Job were righteous—and Scripture informs us that they were—then this was only possible by the working of God. They receive salvation through Christ, even without explicitly confessing faith in him.

Moreover, in these kinds of cases, the gift of saving faith was obviously bestowed *apart from water Baptism.* It would be wrong therefore to insist that the New Testament maintains that only those who enter the waters of Baptism can be saved. When one of the two thieves crucified with Jesus expresses faith in him, Jesus does not inform him that salvation is impossible because he lacks Baptism. Jesus says to the thief, "Truly, I say to you, today you will be with me in Paradise" (Luke 23:43).

Salvation comes first and foremost through the gift of faith. In light of this, the Church teaches, "*God has bound salvation to the sacrament of Baptism, but he himself is not bound by his sacraments*" (*Catechism* §1257). Christ commands the disciples to baptize all peoples (Matthew 28:19) and the New Testament does link salvation to this sacrament (1 Peter 3:21). Baptism is the ordinary means by which we are initiated into the life of faith. The *Catechism* says, "The Church does not know of any means other than Baptism that assures entry into eternal beatitude" (*Catechism* §1257). For these reasons, the Church does not forget Jesus's command to baptize (Matthew 28:19). Nevertheless, it would be wrong to insist that those who have never been baptized cannot be saved.

In the book of Acts, we read about a Gentile named Cornelius, a Roman centurion, whose prayers and acts of generosity to the poor are described as an acceptable sacrifice to God. Cornelius summons Peter and asks to be baptized but, as Thomas Aquinas points out, *he already has the gift of faith.* In fact, the Spirit is already poured out *prior* to Baptism. From this Aquinas concludes that forgiveness of sins is already granted in so far as a person explicitly or implicitly desires

Baptism. This desire can only come from God's grace. Before receiving Baptism, then, Cornelius and others like him received grace and virtues by means of faith. After Baptism, however, Aquinas states, ". . . they receive a yet greater fulness of grace and virtues."[7]

### Salvation through the Body of Christ

What do we make then of the ancient doctrine that there is "no salvation outside the Church"? The formula seems to suggest that only Catholic Christians can be saved. In the mid-twentieth century, controversy erupted when the chaplain of Harvard, Fr. Leonard Feeney, insisted on reading the phrase in this way. In Feeney's view, the expression excludes from salvation all those who are not formal members of the Catholic Church.

Feeney's view was explicitly rejected by the Church. After refusing to heed the warnings of Church authorities, Feeney was finally excommunicated in 1953 for promoting what was seen as a dangerous misinterpretation of Church doctrine. Although he was reconciled to the Church before the end of his life, Feeney's explanation of the phrase "no salvation outside the Church" was deficient. The *Catechism,* the official compendium of Catholic teaching, rightly opposes it.[8]

For one thing, earlier popes and authorities who used the phrase did not necessarily insist that non-baptized Catholics could not be saved. One pope who famously used the formula, Pope Innocent III (d. 1216), also taught that a non-baptized Jew who came to faith in Christ on his deathbed would not be damned, even if he failed to be baptized.[9] More recently, Pope Pius IX offered a more developed reflection on the salvation of the non-baptized. In 1863, he taught:

---

7   *Summa Theologiae,* III q. 69 art. 4 ad 2.

8   The most comprehensive treatment of the topic is Francis Sullivan, *Salvation Outside the Church? Tracing the History of the Catholic Response* (Eugene: Wipf & Stock, 2002).

9   Innocent III, *De Homine Qui* (September 22, 1208).

> . . . those who suffer from invincible ignorance with regard to our
> most holy religion, by carefully keeping the natural law and its
> precepts, which have been written by God in the hearts of all, by
> being disposed to obey God and to lead a virtuous life, can, by the
> power of divine light and grace, attain eternal life.[10]

Feeney's position is obviously inconsistent with Pius's teaching.

Therefore, the *Catechism* explains the doctrine of "no
salvation outside of the church" this way: "Re-formulated
positively, it means that all salvation comes from Christ the
Head through the Church which is his Body" (§846). It goes
on to affirm that "many elements of sanctification and truth"
can be found in non-Catholic Christian communities. It even
states that these communities can be used by God "as means of
salvation," even though their "power derives from the fullness
of grace and truth that Christ has entrusted to the Catholic
Church" (§819). It reiterates that ". . . all these blessings come
from Christ and lead to him and are in themselves calls to
'Catholic unity'" (§819).

Moreover, according to Catholic teaching, non-Christians
also can be saved even if they do not explicitly recognize
Jesus as Lord. Again, recall that Abraham was saved without
knowing the name of the Messiah. In such cases, St. Thomas
Aquinas speaks of an "implicit" faith.[11] Drawing on his
thinking, something similar might be said for non-Christians
who are saved.[12]

### God Works through Others

"No salvation outside the Church" upholds, then, that God
has created us for community. As the poet John Donne rightly
observed, "No man is an island." By nature, human beings

---

10    Pius IX, *Quanto Conficiamur Moerore* (August 10, 1863), §7.

11    *Summa Theologiae*, IIa-IIae, q. 2 art. 5 resp.

12    For a discussion, see Ralph Martin, *Will Many Be Saved? What Vatican II Actually Teaches and Its Implications for the New Evangelization* (Grand Rapids: Eerdmans, 2012), 31–53.

are, as the philosopher Aristotle put it, "social animals."[13] It is no wonder, then, that life comes to each of us *through other people*. This is true of biological life, but it is also true of the supernatural life that we receive by grace.

This is exemplified in the sacraments. You cannot baptize yourself. This expresses a fundamental truth about salvation—it is not *self*-improvement. As we have seen, God saves us by his own initiative of grace.

But God also saves us *from* isolation. God willed to save us through *others*. Being saved is necessarily communal—it involves union not only with Christ but also with his mystical body, the Church. Whether or not they realize it, those who are saved never receive salvation in a way disconnected from all those who are also united to Christ.

When Catholics talk about salvation, they can often fall into the trap of speaking of it in ways that mirror non-Catholic approaches. Salvation becomes primarily about a "personal relationship" and the communal dimension of salvation, specifically the role of the Church, becomes just an "add-on." Yet, according to the New Testament authors, *Christ saves us for communion with the whole body*. The Church cannot simply be "stapled on" to an account of salvation like an addendum. A fully Catholic explanation of salvation recognizes that the Church is, to quote Vatican II, "an instrument for the redemption of all"[14] and is "the universal sacrament of salvation."[15]

If the Church's place in the plan of salvation is not fully appreciated, it can be reduced to nothing more than a social obligation. Rather than seeking to be united to the body, one simply "church hops" until one finds a place where one is told whatever one wants to hear. One is challenged only to the

---

13    Aristotle, *Politics*, I.2.
14    Vatican II, *Lumen Gentium*, no. 9.
15    Vatican II, *Lumen Gentium*, no. 48.

extent one cares to be. Believers become "customers" who seek to *be served* rather than to *serve*.

Finally, the Church's place in Christ's salvific work is especially necessary to emphasize in an age where Church scandals are a major problem. When members, especially Church leaders, are found guilty of egregious sin, the tendency can be to reduce the Church to a mere human institution. This must be fiercely resisted. The true identity of the Church is not coterminous with the failure of her members. Such scandals are the result of the members' rejection of their vocation and they do not manifest the Church's true identity. If the Church is reduced to nothing more than a political party—or an aggregate of opposing ones—such sins are viewed as permissible, even acceptable; scandal and politics go hand-in-hand. In other words, attempts to purify the Church from scandal will never succeed if we only see it as a human institution.

Instead, we should recall what Christ's love for his Church looks like and the lengths to which he went to realize his purpose for her. As Ephesians tells us:

> Husbands, love your wives, as Christ loved the church and gave himself up for her, that he might sanctify her, having cleansed her by the washing of water with the word, that he might present the church to himself in splendor, without spot or wrinkle or any such thing, that she might be holy and without blemish. (Ephesians 5:25–27)

Christ gave all he had to save us through his Church. We should give no less, loving him by working for the good of his whole body with the help of his grace.

# 5

# Not Just a Legal Transaction

We know that in everything God works for good with
those who love him, who are called according to his
purpose. For those whom he foreknew he also predestined
to be conformed to the image of his Son, in order that he
might be the first-born among many brethren.

—Romans 8:28–29

As fire transforms into itself everything it touches, so
the Holy Spirit transforms into the divine life whatever
is subjected to his power.

—*Catechism of the Catholic Church* §1127

As soon as I saw the flashing lights in my rearview mirror, I
knew the police officer had me. He walked up to my window
and showed me what his radar gun had registered. I did not
need to look. I was sure I had exceeded the posted speed limit
by more than twenty miles per hour. I had no excuse. I had
been listening to an up-tempo song while driving on an open
road and simply lost track of how fast I was going. As he sat
in his patrol car and wrote me up, I kicked myself; surely this
would hurt my insurance rate.

When he returned to my window, he explained that I
would need to fill out a form online and pay a fee. He then
offered some news I found rather astonishing: this would not

in any way affect my insurance rate. As he walked away, I looked at the ticket and was stunned to realize that he had marked me down as going only one mile per hour over the speed limit. I was off the hook.

For a lot of Christians, this is a sort analogy for how salvation works. God knows that we are guilty but, out of love, simply looks the other way. The divine judge pronounces us "justified," that is, "just" or "not guilty." Jesus gives to us his legal status as righteous and takes on our guilty status. On the cross, he dies in our place. In this view God's legal decree of justification is counterfactual—we are not truly righteous but only declared to be.

This, however, is not the Catholic understanding of the New Testament's teaching. As we shall see, the New Testament shows us that salvation involves nothing less than being made like Christ. This is why grace is truly amazing—it enables us to become something more than our human nature alone could ever achieve.[1]

## GRACE AS DIVINE INDWELLING

Humanity's struggle with sin should not be underestimated. Paul talks about the way Adam's act of disobedience not only opened the door for sin to enter into the world but enabled it to "reign" (Romans 5:21). In a fallen state, humanity, according to St. Paul, "can will what is right" but "cannot do it" (Romans 7:18). The struggle with sin seems like one we are destined to lose.

Yet, as we have seen, Jeremiah holds out hope for the future. Through the prophet the Lord promises to address

---

1    This chapter offers a popular level summary of the more extensive arguments found in Pitre, Barber, and Kincaid, *Paul*, chapter 5. I especially thank John Kincaid for his help sharpening my presentation.

humanity's "heart problem" by establishing a new covenant. God says, "I will put my law within them, and *I will write it upon their hearts*" (Jeremiah 31:33).

The New Testament insists that this promise has been fulfilled. In Christ, salvation is realized not only because sin is forgiven. Through the Spirit, real change is possible.

### God's Solution to Israel's Heart Problem

In Jeremiah, we hear that God will write the law on human *hearts*. The prophet is picking up a theme Moses talks about frequently in the book of Deuteronomy. Most famously, the heart is mentioned in an injunction in Deuteronomy that Jesus labels "the great and first commandment" (Matthew 22:37–38): ". . . love the LORD your God with *all your heart*, and with all your soul, and with all your might" (Deuteronomy 6:5).

Only a few chapters after issuing this command, Moses implies that the people are unable to carry out this directive, explaining, "*Circumcise therefore the foreskin of your heart*, and be no longer stubborn" (Deuteronomy 10:16). The people are to follow God's law, but they cannot do this until the underlying issue of their heart problem can be solved.

Despite all of this, Moses issues a spectacular promise at the end of the book of Deuteronomy. After describing the future punishments that will come upon the people because of their sin, Moses declares that God will one day restore his people. In doing this, God will finally address the problem behind their disobedience: ". . . the LORD your God will *circumcise your heart and the heart of your offspring, so that you will love the LORD your God* with all your heart and with all your soul, that you may live" (Deuteronomy 30:6). Moses's words indicate that God will intervene to solve Israel's spiritual heart problem. Then God's people will finally be capable of obedience.

The promise of heart transformation emerges in other places in the Bible, most notably in the book of the prophet

Ezekiel, which reveals that heart restoration will be the work of the Spirit. Through Ezekiel, the Lord proclaims:

> A new heart I will give you, and a new spirit I will put within you; and *I will take out of your flesh the heart of stone and give you a heart of flesh.* And *I will put my spirit within you, and cause you to walk in my statutes and be careful to observe my ordinances.* (Ezekiel 36:26–27)

This passage is especially significant because it indicates that keeping God's law will only be possible with the Lord's help. In sending the Spirit, something remarkable will occur—the Lord will *cause* the people to keep the law.

### *The New Covenant and the Gift of the Spirit*

In the New Testament, we learn that these promises have been fulfilled. Paul alludes to Moses's promise of spiritual circumcision when he writes, ". . . *real circumcision is a matter of the heart, spiritual and not literal*" (Romans 2:29). But it is in 2 Corinthians 3 that Paul develops these themes most explicitly.

The Apostle tells the Corinthian believers that they are "a letter from Christ . . . *written not with ink but with the Spirit of the living God, not on tablets of stone but on tablets of human hearts*" (2 Corinthians 3:3). The image of heart-writing is taken from Jeremiah's famous new covenant prophecy (Jeremiah 31:33). Paul, therefore, goes on to speak of himself as a "minister of a *new covenant*" (2 Corinthians 3:6).

Following Ezekiel, Paul also links heart-restoration to the Spirit. Because the Spirit has come through Christ, Paul speaks of the "Spirit of the Son" through whom believers can now be *empowered* to do good works. The Lord's promise to "cause you to walk in my statutes" (Ezekiel 36:27) has now been realized through God's "gift," which, as we have seen, is Paul's way of referring to "grace."

In Galatians 1, grace is specifically linked to Christ's act of self-giving:

> *Grace to you* and peace from God our Father and the Lord Jesus Christ, *who gave himself* for our sins to set us free from the present evil age, according to the will of our God and Father, to whom be the glory forever and ever. (Galatians 1:3–5)

Yet, as Paul later makes clear, Christ's gift of self does not stop at the cross. Through the Spirit, Christ gives himself to believers and remains with them. As Anglican New Testament scholar John Barclay explains, "grace" is nothing less than the "Christ-gift," the gift of *sharing in Christ's life.*[2]

Paul testifies to this in Galatians 2:

> I have been crucified with Christ; *it is no longer I who live, but Christ who lives in me*; and the life I now live in the flesh *I live by faith in the Son of God*, who loved me and *gave himself for me.* I do not nullify *the grace of God*; for if righteousness were through the law, then Christ died to no purpose. (Galatians 2:20–21)[3]

Here the concept of grace is once again closely linked to the notion that Christ "gave himself for me." For Paul, however, the "gift" of Christ's death is ordered to a purpose, namely, Christ living in the believer. Through this "Christ in me" one can live by faith.

Paul says that if righteousness had been possible by the law alone, "then Christ died to no purpose" (Galatians 2:21). The law itself did not make righteousness possible. Christ dies so that his life of faithfulness can be reproduced in us. To quote St. Augustine, "The law was therefore given in order that grace might be sought; grace was given in order that the law might

---

2    See, e.g, Barclay, P*aul and the Gift*, 500–3; 577.

3    RSV-CE adapted.

be fulfilled."[4] Grace thus *empowers* new life, which is nothing less than "Christ in me."

## JUSTIFICATION AND THE PROTESTANT REFORMATION

This brings us to a key dimension of salvation: "justification." The concept is especially prominent in Paul's letters. In large part, it was disagreement over the meaning of this term that divided Christians at the time of the Protestant Reformation. Since that time, Christianity in the West has undergone a radical splintering, with various "denominations" emerging and subdividing. Although advances have been made in finding common ground, justification remains a fiercely debated topic between Catholics and Protestants broadly.

No discussion of "salvation" would be complete without talking about this word. What Catholic teaching emphasizes is this: while "justification" highlights a legal dimension of salvation, God's judgment should not be viewed like the speeding ticket I recounted at the beginning of this chapter. Why? Because God's decree is not contrary to reality. God does what he declares—he declares believers righteous because he *makes* them righteous.

### *Justification as a Legal Decree*
At the outset, it is helpful to explain what "justification" means. Broadly speaking, the language of "justification" relates to being "in the right," "righteous," or "just." In the New Testament, the verb translated "to justify" (Greek *dikaioō*) typically has legal connotations. This sense is clearly present in 1 Corinthians 4. Paul writes, "I am not thereby justified.

---

4    *The Spirit and the Letter*, 34.

It is the Lord who judges me" (1 Corinthians 4:4)."[5] In this verse, to be "justified" is to have right legal standing, that is, to be declared "not guilty" by the divine judge.

With this we come to the heart of the historic disagreement over the meaning of "justification" in Paul. One Protestant perspective—the classical Reformed approach, which is broadly influenced by John Calvin's teachings—insists that when God "justifies" the believer he is only declared "just" or "righteous" in a legal sense. In other words, *this view holds that the believer is "declared" to be righteous without actually being made righteous.* According to this position, the "justified" believer is only righteous in the sense that he or she is "covered" with Christ's righteousness. This is typically explained in terms of a "marvelous exchange": Christ takes the place of sinners, receiving their punishment, and believers assume Christ's legal position of being "not guilty." Various passages in Paul are offered in support of this reading.

Contrary to what some think, Catholic teaching in no way denies that justification involves a legal dimension. But the Catholic doctrine does differ from the Calvinist understanding in a key way. The Calvinist approach holds that when God justifies—that is, when he declares the sinner "righteous"—this relates *only to legal standing*. In other words, in this view, righteousness is about a legal declaration that is *contrary to reality*; justification is not transformation. Catholic doctrine rejects a "purely legal" view of justification and holds that when God declares the sinner "righteous" that decree corresponds to what actually happens—God truly *makes the believer righteous by his grace.* And, as we have seen, "grace" is nothing less than the gift of Christ himself living in us.

---

5    I have adapted the RSV-CE here to make clear that "justification" language is used in the Greek (*dedikaiōmai*). See James B. Prothro, *Both Judge and Justifier* (Tübingen: Mohr Siebeck, 2018), 117–121, and the sources in 117 n. 6.

### Saving Righteousness as Merely Legal

Catholics often misconstrue Protestant views. It is sometimes said that, unlike Catholics, Protestants think that transformation is not part of salvation. This not a fair assessment.

For one thing, "Protestants" are not a monolithic group; there are numerous different non-Catholic Christian perspectives on salvation. One should be careful about talking about *the* Protestant view; there are many different approaches. There are Protestant scholars who insist that justification *does* involve transformation. The approach that sees justification as merely legal represents a particular school of thought which is strongly influenced by John Calvin's teachings. This view is known as the "Reformed" approach. Here I will explain this particular perspective.

We should be clear that the Reformed Protestant perspective holds that transformation is part of salvation. Despite holding that *justification* does not itself involve transformation, the Reformed still insist that transformation belongs to what Paul calls "sanctification." The real debate between Catholics and the Reformed focuses on the meaning of justification.

According to the Reformed view, once one is "justified," one *is* saved. After all, in Romans we read, "For man believes with his heart and so is justified, and he confesses with his lips and so is saved" (Romans 10:10). To be justified is to be saved. Highlighting Paul's teaching that nothing "shall separate us from the love of Christ" (Romans 8:39), the Reformed (and some other Protestants) therefore hold that once a person is saved, salvation can never be lost. If one is "justified," one is saved. Yet being justified *is not defined by being transformed.* The righteousness that saves is only Christ's and Christ's alone, a righteousness that remains outside the believer.

A key passage often quoted in support of the Reformed reading is found in Philippians 3:

I have suffered the loss of all things, and count them as refuse, in order that I may gain Christ and be found in him, not having a righteousness of my own, based on law, but that which is through faith in Christ, the righteousness from God that depends on faith (Philippians 3:8–9)

Here the Apostle Paul maintains in no uncertain terms that saving righteousness is not *from* the believer. Saving righteousness is only found through faith in Christ. On this basis, many Lutheran and Calvinist Protestants conclude that Paul must think that saving righteousness remains *external* to the believer.

Romans 4 is also seen as supporting the idea that justification is purely legal and not transformative. In this chapter, Paul is writing about justification (Romans 4:2) and says, "to one who works, his wages are not reckoned as a gift but as his due" (Romans 4:4). In other words, saving righteousness is given as a grace (gift) because it is not bestowed on the basis of works. Those who are justified by God—those who have saving righteousness—are not justified because of works. Faith, it is said, is merely "counted as" saving righteousness.

The Apostle goes on to cite a Psalm of David, which indicates that God justifies—he "reckons righteous"—without counting sin.

So also David pronounces a blessing upon the man to whom God reckons righteousness apart from works: "Blessed are those whose iniquities are forgiven, and whose sins are covered; blessed is the man against whom the Lord will not reckon his sin." (Romans 4:6–8)

As Paul says, God justifies "the ungodly" (Romans 4:5). From these and other passages, many Protestants conclude that the essence of justification is a legal decree that does not refer to the believer's own transformation.

## TRANSFORMATIVE RIGHTEOUSNESS

How do Catholics view justification? Catholics agree with various Protestant readers on a number of points. We believe that the initial gift of salvation cannot be earned. We believe that God justifies those who are ungodly. We believe that justification is part of salvation. Where we part ways is on the nature of God's decree. Catholic teaching refuses to believe that God would declare something to be true that is, in reality, false. After all, Jesus says to the Father in the Gospel according to John, ". . . your word is truth" (John 17:17). In other words, we Catholics believe that God calls believers righteous because they are truly *made* righteous.

### *Becoming a New Creation*

In response to the Reformation, the Catholic Church solemnly defined the meaning of justification at the Council of Trent (1545–1563). First, the Church affirmed that justification cannot be earned, and that saving righteousness does not come from anything in the believer. The Council affirmed:

> . . . *nothing that precedes justification, neither faith nor works, merits the grace of justification;* for 'if it is by grace, it is no longer on the basis of works; otherwise (as the same apostle says) grace would no longer be grace. [cf. Romans 11:6][6]

The *Catechism* reiterates this teaching, saying, ". . . *no one can merit the initial grace* of forgiveness and justification, at the beginning of conversion" (*Catechism* §2010).

Nevertheless, Catholic teaching *also* holds that when God declares the believer to be "just" he is not speaking in a way that distorts reality; the believer *is* transformed and made

---

6    Council of Trent, Session 6, chapter 8. Cited from Denzinger, *Enchiridion*, 378 [§1532].

righteous by God. Where does the Church get this idea? From St. Paul himself.[7]

Two key passages are relevant here. The first is found in 2 Corinthians. There Paul writes, "For our sake [God] made [Christ] to be sin who knew no sin, so that in [Christ] *we might become the righteousness of God*" (2 Corinthians 5:21). Some have argued that this passage is proof that Christians only become "righteous" in a legal sense because Christ does not actually "become sin." The problem with this view is that it misunderstands Paul's language.

When Paul says that Christ was made "to be sin," he is not saying that Christ "only became sin in a legal sense." In saying Jesus was made to be "sin," Paul is likely describing Jesus as a "sin offering" (*chatta'th*; cf. Leviticus 4:3), that is, a type of sacrifice that effects "atonement." English Bibles use the expression "sin offering" for the sake of clarity, but the word "sacrifice" or "offering" is not usually added; in the Scriptures of Israel, the "sin offering" is literally just called "the sin." Paul's point is not that Jesus "legally" became "sin," but, rather, that Christ offered himself as a "sacrifice for sin." Paul uses similar imagery in Romans 8:3. There he says Christ was sent "for sin," in Greek, *peri harmartias*. This is the same expression that means "sin offering" in the Greek translation of the Old Testament.

In addition, the wider context shows us that Paul holds that believers are truly *changed*. Just before making the statement in 2 Corinthians 5:21 that believers "become the righteousness of God," he maintains, ". . . if anyone is in Christ, *he is a new creation*" (2 Corinthians 5:17). To be "in Christ," then, is to be transformed by him. As many non-Catholic scholars recognize, this makes it virtually impossible to think that Paul's statement that believers "become the righteousness of

---

7    See the fuller treatment in Pitre, Barber, and Kincaid, *Paul*, chapter 5.

God" is referring to a change in legal status that does not include real transformation.

### In the New Adam

A second important passage that indicates justification involves transformation appears in Romans 5. There Paul compares Christ to Adam, contrasting the effects of Christ's obedience with the effects of Adam's disobedience. He writes, "For as by one man's disobedience *many were made sinners*, so by one man's obedience *many will be made righteous*" (Romans 5:19).

As we have seen, Paul held that Adam's sin led all humans to become sinners. But in his view humans did not simply become "sinners" in a legal sense. Paul writes, ". . . death spread to all men because *all men sinned*" (Romans 5:12). In other words, those who are "in Adam" are *actually* sinners. Given this, when Paul teaches that due to Christ's work "many will be made righteous," he cannot be referring to legal standing alone. The whole point of his argument is that Christ causes those who are in him to be *made,* and not simply *declared,* righteous. As we have seen, to be in Christ—the new Adam—is to be a *new creation.*

What of the passages from Philippians 3 and Romans 4 used by those who think saving righteousness is not transformational? First, as regards Philippians 3, Paul's point is *not* that righteousness *remains* external. Rather, his point is that he is not the *origin* of his own righteousness: ". . . *not having a righteousness of my own* . . . but that which is *through faith in Christ, the righteousness from God that depends on faith* (Philippians 3:8–9). To rephrase Paul, there are two kinds of righteousness: one based on one's own obedience to the law and one that has Christ as its origin. The latter depends on trusting in God and not in oneself.

Second, in Romans 4, the idea is that God "justifies" those who are ungodly, not that they *stay* ungodly. Grace is first given to the unworthy as a mercy. Yet once received, grace effects *transformation* so that one *becomes* not only "a new creation" but also "the righteousness of God." As we will further discuss later on (see chapter seven), the Greek word translated "faith" (Greek *pistis*) is not simply "belief" but *faithfulness*. When Paul says the righteous are justified by faith, he is referring to a virtue. They *are* righteous by God's grace and no longer "ungodly."

### Life in Christ

Salvation in Christ entails nothing less than being changed; in him, we are truly remade. This is why Christ's redemptive work is also associated with his resurrection. Although we frequently hear that Jesus "died" to accomplish our salvation, it is worth emphasizing that the resurrection and ascension are also part and parcel of his saving mission. In 1 Corinthians 15, Paul insists, "If Christ has not been raised, your faith is futile, and *you are still in your sins*" (1 Corinthians 15:17). In addition, in Romans 4, Paul explains that Jesus "was put to death for our trespasses and *raised for our justification.*"

As we have seen, Catholic teaching holds that Christ "reveals man to man"—he shows us what it means to be human.[8] The resurrection is an essential aspect of redemption since it makes clear that humanity is meant to be glorified. Through the power of the Spirit, Christ's human nature is not only "restored" to life, it is also *glorified*. In this, Christians are to see to what they have been called—new life, a life that transcends what human nature can achieve on its own.

To be in Christ is to be more than "forgiven;" it is to be *elevated* and *transformed*. Paul even speaks of salvation as being "conformed to the image of [God's] son" (Romans 8:29). To be saved is to share in the very sonship of the Son. This occurs

---

8    Vatican II, *Gaudium Et Spes*, §22.

through a gift, "grace," which is more than divine "favor." Grace is not simply God's "positive" disposition to humanity. Rather, it is life in the Son, or, as the *Catechism* puts it, "Grace is a *participation in the life of God.* It introduces us into the intimacy of Trinitarian life" (§1997).

Justification for Catholics *is* a legal decree. The divine judge declares us "righteous." But the judge in this case also does what he declares; his decree coheres with reality. As John Henry Newman observed, God effects what he declares (cf. Isaiah 55:10–11).[9] When God says at creation, "Let there be light," there *is* light (Genesis 1:3). Likewise, in the "new creation," when God pronounces the sinner "justified," he is *made* righteous.

As Paul says, Christ is "our righteousness" (1 Corinthians 1:30)—justification or "righteousness" is a result of sharing in the life of the Son. This fact must not be downplayed or minimized. If we do that, our bad theology can have dangerous consequences. It can cause us to assume that salvation is not really connected to being faithful to our spouses, attentive to our parents and children, loyal to our friends, and honest with our employers. But the New Testament authors are clear: salvation is about becoming "conformed to the image of [God's] Son"—and this begins in this life. Being saved means *not* living in sin; it means living as Jesus told us to: ". . . be perfect, as your heavenly Father is perfect" (Matthew 5:48).

Is this directive possible? No—at least, not by our own power. But, as Jesus says, ". . . with God all things are possible" (Matthew 19:26). And that is the point of grace—it makes it possible for our humanity not only to be "healed" and "perfected," but also for our nature to be elevated beyond its capacity. As we will see in our next chapter, we are called to *participate* in the work of our salvation.

---

9    John Henry Newman, *Lectures on the Doctrine of Justification,* 3d ed. (New York: Longmans, Green, and Co., 1990), 81–82.

## 6

# Not a Spectator Sport

Therefore, my beloved, as you have always obeyed, so now, not only as in my presence but much more in my absence, *work out your own salvation* with fear and trembling; *for God is at work in you*, both to will and to work for his good pleasure.

—Philippians 2:12–13

Christ's gift of salvation offers us the grace necessary to persevere in the pursuit of the virtues. Everyone should always ask for this grace . . .

—*Catechism of the Catholic Church* §1811

As a father, I have come to discover that by the time my children are around seven years old they generally have gone through two stages. In the first stage, they seek to imitate me. They mimic silly faces or sounds I make. They try to wear my shoes and clothes. Even if I am doing a chore, such as cleaning, they somehow want to look like they are doing some work too.

But my children's desire to imitate eventually gives way to a desire to *participate*. They want to actually *do* whatever it is I am doing. They ask to be my "helper." The older kids want to put the younger kids to bed, or bathe them, or locate items for me while we are shopping at the supermarket. Imitation is no longer enough. They know the difference between imitation and participation—now they want to be part of the action.

The New Testament often talks about the importance of *imitating* Christ. Ephesians, for example, states, ". . . *be imitators of God*, as beloved children. And *walk in love, as Christ loved us and gave himself up for us*" (Ephesians 5:1–2). Nevertheless, the New Testament also emphasizes that salvation involves more than just imitation. According to the New Testament, salvation involves both imitating *and* participating in the life of the divine Son.

Salvation is not simply a "spectator sport." To continue the metaphor, Christ does not instruct us to simply sit in the grandstands. He empowers us to take the field with him and share in his victory with him.

With this in mind we come to another issue that has divided Protestant and Catholic Christians: the role of good works. To be sure, many non-Catholic Christians affirm that good works are one way or another a necessary part of salvation. What often divides Catholics and Protestants is the question of *how* this is the case. Many Christians hold that while good works are necessary, good works *themselves* are not salvific. They argue that good works are *evidence of* saving faith, but that good works do not themselves contribute to one's salvation.

The Catholic belief that good works actually have saving value is sometimes said to detract from the work of Christ. Why must we *add* to Christ's work? Is his work not enough? To say the believer's works have a redemptive role would seem to ignore the New Testament's teaching about grace. After all, as we have noted, Ephesians teaches, ". . . by grace you have been saved through faith; and this is not your own doing, it is the gift of God—not because of works, lest any man should boast" (Ephesians 2:8–9). How then can the good works of the believer have redemptive value in light of this?

In this chapter we will take up this important question. Furthermore, we will explain the spiritual dangers that can lurk behind attempts to downplay the redemptive value of good works. As we shall see, understanding the New Testament's teaching about the role of works is vitally important for recognizing what salvation fully entails.

## JUDGMENT BY WORKS

The Bible affirms the role of good works in various places. What must always be remembered, however, is that such works are only possible because of union with Christ. The believer's works have salvific value because, in the final analysis, such works are ultimately the works of Christ himself. Our good works do not "add" to Christ's work because they are part of it; they are the result of "Christ who lives in me" (Galatians 2:20).

### *Justified by Works and Not by Faith Alone*
Scripture insists that God will judge each person according to his deeds. Consider the following passages. For example, Paul himself writes, "For we must all appear before the judgment seat of Christ, so that each one may receive good or evil, *according to what he has done in the body*" (2 Corinthians 5:10). Likewise, in the book of Revelation, Jesus announces, "I am he who searches mind and heart, and I will give to each of you *as your works deserve*" (Revelation 2:23).[1]

That works will be the essential criterion of judgment on the last day is emphasized by Jesus throughout the Gospels. Most famously, the role of works at the final judgment is affirmed in Matthew 25, where Jesus speaks of his second

---

1   See also, e.g., Romans 2:6; 1 Peter 1:17.

coming. When the righteous are welcomed into the kingdom, they are told why they have gained admittance to eternal life:

> . . . for I was hungry and you gave me food, I was thirsty and you gave me drink, I was a stranger and you welcomed me, I was naked and you clothed me, I was sick and you visited me, I was in prison and you came to me. (Matthew 25:35–36)

The righteous are surprised by this and ask when they did these things for him. Jesus explains, "Truly, I say to you, as you did it to one of the least of these my brethren, you did it to me" (Matthew 25:40). Furthermore, Jesus goes on to declare that those who did not perform such works will "go away into eternal punishment" (Matthew 25:46). Jesus could not be any clearer: good works are the basis for the final judgment.

The epistle of James is even more explicit about the importance of good works: "What does it profit, my brethren, if a man says he has faith but has not works? Can his faith save him?" (James 2:14). Here we see that faith alone cannot save. Going on, James insists that one cannot be justified by "faith alone":

> You see that *a man is justified by works and not by faith alone*. And in the same way *was not also Rahab the harlot justified by works* when she received the messengers and sent them out another way? For as the body apart from the spirit is dead, so *faith apart from works is dead*. (James 2:24–26)

The rhetorical question concerning Rahab—"was not also Rahab the harlot justified by works?"—is obviously to be answered in the affirmative. James teaches that she was, in fact, justified by *works*.

Concerned that this somehow contradicts Paul's teaching that one is "justified by faith apart from works of law" (Romans 3:28), some have argued that James could not mean what it sounds like he means. James is reinterpreted as teaching that saving faith merely *reveals* itself in good works. In other words, as some non-Catholic Christians have been known to put it, "faith alone saves but saving faith is never alone." They acknowledge that saving faith is never without works. Nonetheless, they maintain, "faith alone" is what saves.

Others take a different tactic. They explain that James says, "*You see* that a man is justified by works," because he is only concerned here with how justification *appears* to take place, that is, how it seems to unfold from a human perspective. But, again, James's point is clear: works *themselves* are justifying.

How is this possible? Because James is talking about works that are performed by one who is in union with Christ. He is talking to fellow believers, who have been "brought forth by the word of truth that we should be a kind of first fruits of his creatures" (James 1:18).

The New Testament authors probably did not believe they needed to spell out that good works were ultimately the result of the working of God in the believer. Ancient Jews did not necessarily see divine and human actors as somehow separable or in competition with one another. They did not automatically assume one had to *either* attribute good works to God or a human. That God would *enable* obedience was already clear from books like Ezekiel: "I will put my spirit within you, and *cause you to walk in my statutes*" (Ezekiel 36:27).

In other words, authors like James, Matthew, and Paul knew that works cannot, simply speaking, merit God's mercy and assistance. Once one is united to Christ by grace, however, one's works can become salvific because Christ lives in the believer. This idea of union with Christ is seen in multiple places in the New Testament.

### Christ Who Lives in Me

Let us return to Jesus's teaching in Matthew 25. It is important to observe that Christ assumes that *believers are somehow united to him.* Jesus teaches that what is done to his "brethren" is actually done to him: "Truly, I say to you, *as you did it to one of the least of these my brethren, you did it to me*" (Matthew 25:40). On the last day, he tells the righteous, "You gave *me* food . . . you gave *me* drink . . . you welcomed *me* . . . you clothed *me* . . . you visited *me* . . . you came to *me*." Jesus is united to believers.

Various other sayings of Jesus in the Gospels point to this notion that believers are united to Christ. In Luke 10:16, Christ says, "*He who hears you hears me, and he who rejects you rejects me.*" In the Fourth Gospel, Jesus teaches, "I am the vine, you are the branches. He who abides in me, and I in him, he it is that bears much fruit, for apart from me you can do nothing" (John 15:5).

Christ's indwelling in believers is especially emphasized by Paul. Christ is actively working *through* believers by grace. He insists, ". . . it is no longer I who live, but *Christ who lives within me*" (Galatians 2:20). Likewise, in Philippians, he writes:

> *Therefore*, my beloved, as you have always *obeyed*, so now, not only as in my presence but much more in my absence, *work out your own salvation with fear and trembling; for God is at work in you,* both to will and to work for his good pleasure. (Philippians 2:12–13)

Believers are capable of participating in their own salvation because *God* is at work within them.

The Apostle even indicates that we receive grace in vain if we fail to respond with good works: "Working together with him, then, we entreat you *not to accept the grace of God in vain*" (2 Corinthians 6:1). God's gift of grace comes with expectations—good works, which the gift of Christ's presence in the believer makes possible. Since grace empowers, to refuse to respond to it is to "accept the grace of God in vain." To resist cooperation with God's work is to thwart the purpose of grace.

### Doing the Impossible

To reiterate, achieving salvation through good works is not simply difficult; humanly speaking, it is impossible apart from grace. Jesus underscores this idea in his encounter with a rich man in Matthew 19. Let us take a careful look at the story.

The rich man asks Jesus: "Teacher, *what good must I do*, to have eternal life?" (Matthew 19:16; cf. Mark 10:17). Strikingly, Jesus does not correct the man for thinking works are necessary to enter eternal life. When Jesus reminds him of the commandments, the young man insists that he has kept them. Remarkably, Jesus accepts this answer. In the end, he tells the man, "*If you would be perfect*, go, sell what you possess and give to the poor, and *you will have treasure in heaven*; and come, follow me" (Matthew 19:21). Some have suggested that Jesus here is giving a standard Jewish answer and is not speaking directly to his disciples. Yet Matthew's presentation makes no such distinction (cf. Matthew 28:19–20).

Others have argued that the rich man's salvation itself is not at stake in the story. This is unconvincing. After the man declines Jesus's invitation and walks away from him, Jesus says that it is "hard for a rich man *to enter the kingdom of God*" (Matthew 19:23–24). The disciples then marvel at Jesus's words and exclaim, "Who then can be *saved* (*sōthēnai*)?" (Matthew 19:25). This leads Jesus to talk about "inheriting *eternal life*" (Matthew 19:29). Throughout the passage there is no doubt that the issue at hand is the man's very salvation. This is how the *Catechism* understands the passage (§308 and §1058).

When the disciples marvel at Jesus's words to the rich man, he responds: "With men this is impossible, but with God all things are possible" (Matthew 19:26). The perfection Jesus asks for is something beyond human perfection. Jesus calls his disciples to be perfect "as your heavenly Father is perfect" (Matthew 5:48). This, obviously, is an entirely unattainable goal for human beings. Nevertheless, Jesus emphasizes that God makes it possible for us to attain it. With God's help, somehow, *we can do the impossible.*

## SALVATION AS COMPENSATION AND THE CONCEPT OF MERIT

Earlier we looked at the way "redemption" draws on financial imagery. Sin is depicted as a "debt" in Scripture. Yet this is only half of the equation. If sins are a "debt," good deeds can be described as a kind of "credit." Of course, gaining "credit" is only possible by means of God's grace, that is, by union with Christ. Nonetheless, the language highlights the very real salvific value of the good works accomplished with God's help. It is worth, therefore, looking at this dimension of the New Testament's teaching more closely.

### *Your Reward Will Be Great in Heaven*

Given that sins are viewed as debts, it is not surprising to find that the reverse is also true—good deeds will be "reimbursed." One of the earliest texts suggesting this perspective is Proverbs 19:17: "He who is kind to the poor lends to the Lord, and *he will repay him for his deed*" (Proverbs 19:17). Performing good deeds will lead to divine repayment.

The book of Daniel carries this further, suggesting that the "credit" gained by good deeds can offset the "debt" incurred by sin. When King Nebuchadnezzar is informed that he will be punished because of his evil ways, the king also learns of a way to mitigate the penalty he has incurred: *almsgiving,* that is, giving to the poor. The prophet Daniel urges Nebuchadnezzar, ". . . *redeem* your sins by practicing *righteousness,* and your iniquities by *showing mercy to the oppressed,* that there may perhaps be a lengthening of your tranquility" (Daniel 4:27).[2] As Old Testament scholar Gary Anderson shows, the word translated "righteousness" (*tsidqâ*) was often used to describe almsgiving.[3] Daniel is therefore advising Nebuchadnezzar to pay off the debt of his sin by giving to the poor.

By Jesus's day, it was understood that good deeds like almsgiving not only gained a kind of spiritual "credit," they were also understood to be "deposited" in a sort of heavenly bank account or "treasury." This is evident in the books of Tobit and Sirach. These books show us how ancient Jews in and around the time of Christ thought about the value of good works.

> . . . if you do what is true, *your ways will prosper through your deeds.* Give alms from your possessions to all who live uprightly, and do not let your eye begrudge the gift when you make it. *Do not turn your face away from any poor man, and the face of God will not be turned away from you.* If you have many possessions, make your gift from them in proportion; if few, do not be afraid to give according to the little you have. So *you will be laying up a good treasure for yourself against the day of necessity.* For *charity delivers from death and keeps you from entering the darkness;* and *for all who practice it charity is an excellent offering in the presence of the Most High.* (Tobit 4:6–11)

> *Whoever honors his father atones for sins,* and *whoever glorifies his mother is like one who lays up treasure.* . . . For kindness to a father will not be forgotten, and *against your sins it will be credited to you;* in the day of your affliction it will be remembered in your favor; as frost in fair weather, *your sins will melt away.* (Sirach 3:3–4, 14–15)

---

2    RSV-CE adapted. Many English translations render this passage with something like "*break off* your sins," but it is better translated as "*redeem* your sins." See Gary Anderson, *Sin: A History* (New Haven: Yale University Press, 2009), 135–51.

3    See Anderson, *Sin,* 221 n. 10.

By the first century, then, Jews viewed good deeds through this lens of "heavenly economics."

Before moving on, one important clarification is in order. Passages such as these should not be understood as suggesting that good works like almsgiving *force* God's hand. For Jewish writers, God is not *required* to reward anyone. The heavenly economics these texts envision should not be viewed in mechanical terms. When the biblical sources employ this kind of financial imagery, the underlying assumption is that good works are presented to God for approval; God *may* reward them. The hope of blessing is rooted in confidence in God's love and mercy. It is understood that God *wants* us to learn generosity and gain forgiveness. As Anderson writes, "When it works, it is because of God's gracious decision to honor the merits of the saints."[4]

### The Heavenly Treasury and Salvation as a Wage

Jesus's teaching in the Gospels bears the unmistakable stamp of these Jewish traditions. For example, when the rich young man asks Jesus what he needs to do to be saved, Jesus speaks of the notion of a heavenly treasury: ". . . sell what you possess and *give to the poor*, and you will have *treasure in heaven*" (Matthew 19:21). Likewise, in the Gospel according to Luke, Jesus states: "Sell your possessions, and *give alms*; provide yourselves with *purses that do not grow old, with a treasure in the heavens that does not fail*, where no thief approaches and no moth destroys" (Luke 12:33).

Jesus's use of financial imagery is more common than we often realize. English translations often mask it. This is especially the case in places where Jesus speaks of salvation in terms of a "reward." Take, for instance, this lesson from the Sermon on the Mount:

---

4    Gary Anderson, *Christian Doctrine and the Old Testament* (Grand Rapids: Baker Academic, 2017), 199.

> Beware of practicing your piety before men in order to be seen by them; for then *you will have no reward* [Greek *misthos*] from your Father who is in heaven. Thus, when you give alms, sound no trumpet before you, as the hypocrites do in the synagogues and in the streets, that they may be praised by men. Truly, I say to you, *they have received their reward* [Greek *misthos*]. But when you give alms, do not let your left hand know what your right hand is doing, so that your alms may be in secret; and *your Father who sees in secret will reward* [Greek *apodidōmi*] *you*. (Matthew 6:1–4)

Today, the English word "reward" is rarely used in the sense of an employer/employee or creditor/debtor relationship. One receives a "reward" for finding a lost puppy, not as one's *wage* or as financial compensation for labor. Yet previous generations of English speakers used the term "reward" in just that way, that is, as referring to a "payment."[5] The Greek terms Jesus uses often have this meaning.

That the word translated "reward" means remuneration can be seen in the Parable of the Workers found in Matthew 20. Jesus here compares the kingdom of heaven to laborers who are paid at the end of a long workday. Jesus explains, "And when evening came, the owner of the vineyard said to his steward, 'Call the laborers and pay [Greek *apodidōmi*] them their *wages*, beginning with the last, up to the first'" (Matthew 20:8). The Greek word translated "wages" is *misthos,* the very same term that is usually rendered with the English word "reward." The context makes it clear that the word refers specifically to financial remuneration for services rendered. In fact, the word translated "pay" is often rendered "rewarded" in other contexts, as in Matthew 6:4, which we quoted above.

In other places in the Gospels, *misthos,* "wages," is translated "reward." This is unfortunate. In doing this, translations obscure or downplay Jesus's use of financial language to describe

---

5    Nathan Eubank, *Wages of Cross-Bearing and Debt of Sin* (Berlin: De Gruyter, 2013), 68–70.

salvation. In short, when Jesus speaks about receiving a "reward," he literally usually means "compensation" or "payment."

Nevertheless, the notion of salvation as a "recompense" or as "remuneration" is not always lost in translation. The RSV accurately captures the economic resonances of Jesus's words in Matthew 16:27, where Jesus announces: "For the Son of man is to come with his angels in the glory of his Father, and then *he will repay* (Greek *apodidōmi*) every man for what he has done." The RSV also accurately conveys Jesus's meaning in the Parable of the Unforgiving Servant, where he describes the final judgment as a "settling of *accounts*" (cf. Matthew 18:23).

Therefore, to say that works *themselves* are not saving flies in the face of what Jesus says. Catholic teaching uses the concept of "merit" to describe this aspect of Scripture's teaching. Broadly speaking, "merit" refers to "recompense owed," which can mean either "reward" or "punishment" (*Catechism* §2006). To be precise, salvation is not just "recompense" in a general sense; Jesus uses the language of *repayment* or *compensation*.

In sum, the good works accomplished by believers are "rewarded" or "paid" with salvation—they *themselves* have salvific value. Why? Because they are truly the work of Christ alive in the believer. To claim such works are not to be "rewarded" would be to insist, contrary to Scripture's teaching, that they either are not truly the work of Christ or that some of Christ's own works do not have salvific value.

## THE POWER OF GRACE

Many non-Catholic Christians will object to my discussion, arguing that talking about the role of works undermines the teaching that God's grace is sufficient. I profoundly disagree.

That would only be true if grace and works accomplished in Christ were somehow in competition with one another. In fact, in a Catholic approach, recognizing the role of works in salvation only underscores the truly amazing character of grace. In Catholic teaching, grace enables us to do what, on our own power, is truly impossible. If the Catholic view is wrong—and I emphatically do not believe that is the case—it would be because the Catholic teaching holds that grace is *too* amazing.

### The Parable of the Workers

We must be clear that when we speak of "merit" we are talking in a qualified sense. The only reason "merit" is possible is because of grace. Salvation cannot be "earned," simply speaking; God does not "owe" us his mercy. We must guard against viewing merit in terms of a strict *quid pro quo* arrangement. This would be a gross distortion of the New Testament's teaching.

To see this dynamic at work, let us return once again to the Parable of the Workers, which we have already mentioned above. In the story, Jesus compares the kingdom of heaven to laborers who receive their payment at the end of a workday. At the end of the parable something unexpected happens. We learn that those who had worked since morning receive the same wage as those who only worked one hour. The laborers then complain to the householder. The householder responds to them as follows:

> Friend, I am doing you no wrong; did you not agree with me for a denarius? Take what belongs to you, and go; I choose to give to this last as I give to you. Am I not allowed to do what I choose with what belongs to me? Or do you begrudge my generosity? (Matthew 20:13–15)

What is the message of this parable?

Given the way Jesus uses the language elsewhere, the "wage" paid to the laborers is best seen as an image of salvation. For some readers, this is troubling since it implies that salvation can—at least in some sense—be "earned." Attempts have been made to downplay this. Some claim the finale reveals that works are actually irrelevant to salvation. After all, all the laborers receive the same payment despite doing different amounts of work. Along these lines, one commentator argues that the real meaning of the story is that salvation is "all by grace."[6]

As we have seen, Catholic teaching in no way rejects the priority of grace. It affirms Paul's insistence that salvation is not earned. The *Catechism* therefore teaches that salvation is "pure grace" (§2011).

Nevertheless, it is hard to argue that Jesus tells the story to minimize the value of works. As Nathan Eubank points out, in the story everyone who is paid does *some* work—no one is paid for *not* working.[7] If Jesus's goal was to indicate that works are not necessary for salvation, he would have told a story different than this one. Instead of hiring people to work, the vineyard owner would have gone through the town and paid everyone without any conditions whatsoever. That is *not* what happens though. As it stands, the story reveals that the wage of salvation is in some sense "earned."

### Divine Generosity

Still—and this must be emphasized—the Parable of the Workers shows us that salvation (payment) is not simply doled out according to a cold calculus in which works are rigidly quantified by God. The context of the story is particularly important. It immediately follows the account of

---

6    R. T. France, *The Gospel of Matthew* (Grand Rapids: Eerdmans, 2007), 752.

7    See Eubank, *Wages of Cross-Bearing,* 94–99. My presentation here draws heavily from his insightful work.

Jesus's encounter with the rich young man who walked away sad because he was unable to part with his many possessions (Matthew 19:16–22). As we pointed out before, the man tells Jesus that he has kept all God's commandments. Jesus instructs him to sell all he has and give the money to the poor. Recognizing Jesus's incredibly difficult demand, the disciples exclaim: "Who then can be saved?" (Matthew 19:25)

Read in isolation, the story may seem to indicate this man is damned; he has not done "enough." The Parable of the Workers, however, gives us hope for him. By placing the Parable of the Workers immediately after Jesus's encounter with this rich man, Matthew warns us against writing him off. The laborers who come at the end of the day work for only an hour, but still receive the full wage. God is able to do much with only a little from us.

In sum, according to Matthew, salvation—"wages"—are paid in association with work, *but not in strict proportion to it.* The story illustrates the necessity of works, while also emphasizing God's mercy. In the end, God pays out far more than what is actually "earned." Good works and God's graciousness are not contradictory ideas.

### *Apart from Me You Can Do Nothing*
To reiterate, the "merit" of believers' works is, according to Catholic teaching, *only* possible because such works are ultimately those performed by Christ empowering the believer. The *Catechism,* reaffirming the teaching of the Council of Trent, insists on this:

> *The charity of Christ is the source in us of all our merits* before God. Grace, by uniting us to Christ in active love, ensures the supernatural quality of our acts and consequently their merit before God and before men. The saints have always had a lively awareness that their merits were pure grace. (§2011)

Going on, the *Catechism* illustrates this teaching with a beautiful quotation from St. Thérèse of Lisieux,

> After earth's exile, I hope to go and enjoy you in the fatherland, but I do not want to lay up merits for heaven. I want to work for your *love alone*. . . . In the evening of this life, I shall appear before you with empty hands, for I do not ask you, Lord, to count my works. All our justice is blemished in your eyes. I wish, then, to be clothed in your own *justice* and to receive from your *love* the eternal possession of *yourself.* (*Catechism* §2011)

All of this reflects Jesus's teaching in the Gospel according to John: ". . . apart from me you can do nothing" (John 15:5).

In other words, the initial gift of God that empowers us to do saving works is not earned. As the letter to the Ephesians says, "For by grace you have been saved through faith; and this is not your own doing, it is the gift of God—not because of works, lest any man should boast" (Ephesians 2:8–9). Yet this grace is given *to enable us to do works that have redemptive value.* Ephesians therefore thus quickly adds: "*For we are his workmanship, created in Christ Jesus for good works,* which God prepared beforehand, *that we should walk in them*" (Ephesians 2:10). By grace we are enabled to do the works *God* has prepared for us—our works are the Lord's.

St. Augustine articulates the Catholic understanding of all of this in one simple phrase. Speaking of the final judgment, he writes, "*Then God will crown not so much thy merits, as his own gifts.*"[8] The works that are rewarded are ultimately those accomplished by God's grace in believers.

To reject this notion is to pervert the biblical teaching and to reduce salvation to a "spectator sport," in which Christ essentially tells believers to "sit it out." This aspect of the New Testament's message is important because it speaks to

---

8    *Sermon 120.*

Christ's desire to bring about a real restoration of the dignity of human nature. The Savior does not simply come and do the work *for us;* he also invites us to have a true share in his redemptive mission. This is why good works are necessary—without them we are not truly "conformed to the image of [God's] Son" (Romans 8:29).

What consequences are there for failing to recognize this truth? First, it can lead to a sort of spiritual despair. We could be tempted to conclude that our works have little consequence. If they are only "evidence" of our faith and do not truly "count" towards salvation, they appear to have little actual value beyond validating faith. This can lead us to underestimate what good works performed in union with Christ can accomplish—they can have truly redemptive effects.

Second, if works are primarily seen as necessary for authenticating our faith another danger can arise: works might be performed just for the sake of show. Jesus warns against this danger in Matthew 6: "Beware of practicing your piety before men in order to be seen by them" (Matthew 6:1). If the point of good works is to demonstrate that one truly has "saving faith," the focus shifts to the individual rather than making Christ's role central. The danger here is a profound one. One can fall into the trap of performing good works to ensure that one knows whether or not one will actually be saved—or to impress others.

Catholics can easily fall into these traps. Here we simply need to emphasize what every Catholic should already know: grace empowers good works. Grace is so amazing it actually enables us to *share* in Christ's work. We must not boast in them for they are only made possible by Christ. Through the Spirit, Christ dwells in the believer and continues his work. Specifically, this has important implications for understanding suffering, the topic to which we now turn to examine.

# 7

# Not Simply a Moment

And [God's] gifts were . . . to equip the saints for the work of ministry, for building up the body of Christ, until we all attain to the unity of the faith and of the knowledge of the Son of God, to mature manhood, to the measure of the stature of the fulness of Christ; so that we may no longer be children . . . Rather, speaking the truth in love, we are to grow up in every way into him who is the head, into Christ.

—Ephesians 4:11, 12–15

The Church which is the Body of Christ participates in the offering of her Head. . . . The lives of the faithful, their praise, sufferings, prayer, and work, are united with those of Christ and with his total offering, and so acquire a new value.

—*Catechism of the Catholic Church* §1368

Gloria Gaynor's life changed forever in 1979 when her hit song "I Will Survive" made her a music sensation. In her autobiography, she talks openly about how becoming part of the music scene's "in crowd" led her to the brink of personal destruction. A life of non-stop partying, which was fueled by heavy alcohol and substance abuse, led to the unraveling of her marriage. She felt like she was "sinking into the depths of degradation."

Things began to turn around for her when, after attending a church service, she went home, dusted off an old Bible someone had once given her, and started reading it. "In 1982," she writes, "I got saved." She adds, "I got saved sitting at my own dining room table."

The expression Gaynor consistently uses—"I got saved"—is commonly used among non-Catholic Christians, but it is quite foreign to Catholic piety. As I mentioned in the introduction, Catholics usually conceive of salvation as a *future* reality, namely, as going to "heaven."

It is important to clarify what is meant by this. Heaven is not simply a realm where saints float around on clouds with naked baby angels. Such artistic descriptions are intended to convey the notion of glory and fulfillment.

Heaven is essentially union with God. In a homily, Pope Benedict XVI explained that as Christians we do not look to "a heaven consisting of abstract ideas or even an imaginary heaven created by art, but the heaven of true reality which is God himself. God is heaven. He is our destination."[1] Heaven is nothing less than union with God. Being saved is being in communion with the Triune God. Paul therefore speaks of his death as "to depart and be with Christ" (Philippians 1:23).

Nevertheless, the New Testament does speak of salvation as a reality experienced by believers in this life. For example, in his letter to the Romans, Paul speaks about the day of the resurrection of the dead, saying, ". . . in this hope we *were saved*" (Romans 8:24). It is not entirely unbiblical, then, to talk of salvation in the past tense. In Ephesians, we hear, ". . . by grace *you have been saved*" (Ephesians 2:8).

Yet the terminology "got saved" is not specifically found in the New Testament. Significantly, that language might be seen as emphasizing the idea that salvation is merely a *passive*

---

1    Benedict XVI, Homily for Solemnity of the Assumption (August 15, 2008).

experience. "I *got* saved" seems to suggest that salvation happens to a believer, downplaying any part he or she may play in it. Catholic tradition, as we have seen, upholds the New Testament teaching that, by God's grace, believers participate in Christ's saving work. For example, the Apostle Paul writes, ". . . *work out your own salvation* with fear and trembling; *for God is at work in you,* both to will and to work for his good pleasure" (Philippians 2:12–13). The initial gift of salvation is received apart from works. But this does not exclude the notion of our participation.

In this chapter we will take a closer look at why salvation is described as past, present, and future in Scripture. First, we will see how understanding salvation in terms of sonship helps make sense of these different "tenses" of salvation. Second, we will see how sonship is perfected in suffering. Finally, our conversation will lead us to a doctrine that is frequently misunderstood yet is nonetheless necessary for preserving the New Testament's full teaching about salvation: purgatory.

## SALVATION AS BECOMING CHILDREN OF GOD

We have seen that salvation in the New Testament is more than merely a legal or juridical transaction. Being saved is not just about being declared "not guilty." It is a family matter—we are called by God to become his sons and daughters. Salvation, therefore, is not merely about a discrete moment in time. It also involves growing up.

### *"Being Saved"*

According to the New Testament authors, salvation in Christ occurs in the past, present, *and* future. St. Paul, for example, speaks of salvation as something Christians have *already* experienced: ". . . in this hope we *were saved*" (Romans 8:24).

Likewise, in Ephesians, we read, "For by grace *you have been saved* by faith" (Ephesians 2:8).

How does salvation occur in the life of the believer? In 1 Peter it is explicitly linked to Baptism: "Baptism . . . *now saves you*" (1 Peter 3:21). Paul also links justification—a key dimension of salvation—to Baptism (cf. 1 Corinthians 6:11; Romans 6:1–14).[2] In light of this, a legitimate New Testament response to the question "Are you saved?" would be: "Yes, I was saved at Baptism."

Still, while such an answer would be consistent with the New Testament's message, it would be incomplete. For the biblical writers, salvation in Christ is more than a past event. It *also* refers to something that will take place in the future. In the Gospel of Matthew, Jesus explains, ". . . he who endures to the end *will be saved*" (Matthew 10:22). Paul also describes salvation as a future event in his first letter to the Corinthians where he talks about how the believer "will be saved" at the final judgment (1 Corinthians 3:15).

Finally, we should note that the New Testament indicates salvation has an *ongoing* dimension. The Apostle speaks of "us *who are being saved*" (1 Corinthians 1:18). Similarly, in the book of Acts, we read that "the Lord added to their number day by day *those who were being saved*" (Acts 2:47). Salvation is not merely a past or future event but a continuing reality. How is this case?

### Salvation, Sonship, and Maturity

According to some non-Catholic Christian interpreters, the New Testament presents salvation as a two-step process. One is first "justified." In this view, justification is a one-time event in the life of the believer: God declares what status the believer will have at final judgment. From this follows the process of

---

2    See Isaac Augustine Morales, O.P., "Baptism and Union with Christ," in *"In Christ" in Paul,* eds. Michael J. Thate et al. (Tübingen: Mohr Siebeck, 2014), 157–177.

sanctification, that is, the process of becoming "holy" (Latin *sanctus*). When the New Testament describes salvation as an ongoing process, sanctification, then, is said to be in view.

The problem with this approach is that it flies in the face of the way Paul speaks. In 1 Corinthians, the Apostle states, ". . . you were washed, you were sanctified, you were justified" (1 Corinthians 6:11). Here being "washed"—best read as a reference to Baptism—is linked to both sanctification and justification. For Paul, these are not spoken of as separable realities.[3] Instead, here I would like to offer another explanation for the New Testament's way of speaking about salvation.

As we have seen, salvation in Christ is described in *familial* terms. Those in Christ share in his divine sonship. Paul therefore speaks of salvation as being "called into the *communion* [Greek *koinōnia*] of [God's] Son, Jesus Christ our Lord" (1 Corinthians 1:9). The Apostle even links salvation to "adoption" (Romans 8:23; Galatians 4:5). If this is the case, it is not hard to see why salvation involves a process; children must grow up.

Hebrews 5 gives particular attention to this idea. There we read:

> For though by this time you ought to be teachers, you need some one to teach you again the first principles of God's word. You need milk, not solid food; for every one who lives on milk is unskilled in the word of righteousness, for he is a child. But *solid food is for the mature*, for those who have their faculties trained by practice to distinguish good from evil. (Hebrews 5:12–14)

One who is ignorant of "the first principles of God's word" is "a child" and requires "milk." In other words, believers begin as spiritual infants. Yet Christ wants us to consume "solid

---

3    For more, see Pitre, Barber, and Kincaid, *Paul*, chapter 5.

food." By having their "faculties trained by practice," believers become "mature."

This process of spiritual growth is not merely individualistic. As we have emphasized, the New Testament insists that believers are not saved *separately*. Salvation takes place in communion with others. Ephesians, therefore, speaks of the way the members of the Church grow *together into Christ*. The following quotation is lengthy but merits careful attention:

> And [Christ's] gifts were that some should be apostles, some prophets, some evangelists, some pastors and teachers, to equip the saints for the work of ministry, *for building up the body of Christ*, until we all attain to the unity of the faith and of the knowledge of the Son of God, *to mature manhood, to the measure of the stature of the fulness of Christ*; so that we may *no longer be children*, tossed to and fro and carried about with every wind of doctrine, by the cunning of men, by their craftiness in deceitful wiles. Rather, speaking the truth in love, *we are to grow up in every way into him who is the head, into Christ, from whom the whole body*, joined and knit together by every joint with which it is supplied, when each part is working properly, *makes bodily growth and upbuilds itself in love*. (Ephesians 4:11–16)

This passage indicates that all the members of the body of Christ grow *with one another*. The gifts given to each believer are ultimately intended *for the building up of the whole body*.

In addition, it is crucial to recognize the way this passage from Ephesians 4 also stresses the idea of a mystical union of believers in Christ. Believers are never saved in isolation from one another. What happens to one member of the body of Christ is consequential for the other members as well. This is especially highlighted by the New Testament's teaching regarding the role of suffering, a topic to which we now turn.

## MATURITY THROUGH REDEMPTIVE SUFFERING

Since salvation entails being "conformed to the image of [God's] Son" (Romans 8:29), it should be no wonder that the New Testament insists that believers will suffer as Christ did. Suffering is not an addendum to salvation in the New Testament; it is not merely "evidence" of being saved. According to the biblical authors, saving faith entails participation in Christ's own suffering. Furthermore, the faithful obedience of the members of Christ's body actually benefits others. This is a critical dimension of the New Testament's teaching that requires careful analysis. If we fail to recognize its importance, we run the risk of reducing salvation to mere individualism. In that case we would fail to understand fully why the Church is essential for New Testament salvation.

### *Faith as Co-Crucifixion*

For Paul, faith involves "co-crucifixion." He tells the Galatians, "*I have been crucified with Christ*; it is no longer I who live, but Christ who lives in me; and the life I now live in the flesh *I live by faith* in the Son of God" (Galatians 2:20). In other words, to live by faith is to suffer with Christ.

In Philippians, Paul makes a similar point. He speaks of his to desire to "*gain Christ* and *be found in him*," which, he says, comes "through *faith in Christ*" (Philippians 3:8–9). The Apostle adds that he wishes to "*share his sufferings, becoming like him in his death*, that if possible I may attain the resurrection from the dead" (Philippians 3:8–11).[4] Once again, faith involves "sharing" in the afflictions of Christ.

This aspect of having "faith" is often neglected. For many, "faith" is simply accepting something as true. Yet the Greek word translated "faith," *pistis*, means something more than

---

4   RSV-CE, slightly adapted.

"belief." As one scholar says, in ancient Greek sources, *pistis* is "always a virtue."[5] Faith, therefore, has the connotation of "faithfulness" or "trustworthiness." Paul has this meaning in mind when he writes of "the faithfulness [Greek *pistis*] of God" (Romans 3:3). Paul is not talking about what God "believes." Instead, the Apostle is speaking about God's character—the Father is true to his promises.

The Greek term *pistis* also has the connotation of "obedience." In Romans, Paul talks about the "obedience of faith" (Romans 1:5; 16:26). Here "faith" (Greek *pistis*) means more than just holding a particular belief. "Faith" involves submitting to God's will in trust. Christ himself is the model of this; he was "obedient unto death" (Philippians 2:8). When Paul says that "faith" saves, he does not mean that all one has to do is simply accept the truth of the Gospel message. For Paul, true faith is ultimately sharing in the life-giving sacrificial love of Christ.

### *Suffering as Purification*

In the New Testament we learn that the perfection of human love is found in suffering for others. In the Fourth Gospel, Jesus utters the famous words, "Greater love has no man than this, that a man lay down his life for his friends" (John 15:13). Yet, according to Jesus in the Gospels, this kind of self-giving love is precisely what is required to be saved. Jesus proclaims: "For whoever would save his life will lose it; and *whoever loses his life for my sake, he will save it*" (Luke 9:24; cf. Matthew 16:25; Mark 8:35).

The significance of suffering is more fully developed in Hebrews. We are told, "Although he was a Son, [Jesus] learned obedience through what he suffered; and *being made perfect* he became the source of eternal salvation to all who

---

5    Teresa Morgan, *Roman Faith and Christian Faith* (Oxford: Oxford University Press, 2015), 76.

obey him" (Hebrews 5:8–9). How can the New Testament speak of Jesus's need to be "made perfect"? As the fathers and doctors of the Church clarify, Jesus did not need to "perfect" his divinity. What Jesus perfects is his *human* nature—and this occurs through *suffering*.[6]

The perfective nature of suffering is taught in other ways in Scripture. In particular, the biblical writers use the language of "fire" to describe the way suffering brings about spiritual maturity. This idea is articulated in the book of Sirach:

> My son, if you come forward to serve the Lord,
>     prepare yourself for *trials* . . .
> For *gold is tested in the fire,*
>     and acceptable men in the furnace of humiliation.
> *Put faith* in [God], and he will help you . . . (Sirach 2:1, 5–6)[7]

Suffering, therefore, brings about a kind of *refinement.*

This notion is picked up in 1 Peter 1, where we read: ". . . you may have to suffer various trials, so that *the genuineness of your faith,* more precious than gold which though perishable *is tested by fire,* may redound to praise and glory and honor at the revelation of Jesus Christ" (1 Peter 1:6–7). The letter goes on to explain that suffering is not only possible, it is inevitable for believers: "Beloved, do not be surprised at *the fiery ordeal which comes upon you to prove you,* as though something strange were happening to you. But *rejoice in so far as you share Christ's sufferings,* that you may also rejoice and be glad when his glory is revealed" (1 Peter 4:12–13).

Going on, the letter makes a remarkable claim: "Since therefore Christ suffered in the flesh, arm yourselves with the same thought, for *whoever has suffered in the flesh has ceased from sin*" (1 Peter 4:1). For 1 Peter, suffering brings purification. Elsewhere Paul also talks about the value of suffering this way:

---

6  See *Catechism of the Catholic Church* §609.
7  RSV-CE slightly adapted.

". . . suffering produces endurance, and endurance produces character, and character produces hope, and hope does not disappoint us" (Romans 5:4–5).

In his letter to the Romans, Paul links suffering to glory: "We are children of God, and if children, then heirs, heirs of God and fellow heirs with Christ—*if, in fact, we suffer with him so that we may also be glorified with him*" (Romans 8:16–17).[8] In Paul's teaching, suffering is a kind of prerequisite for glorification. As the book of Acts reports, Paul holds that "through many tribulations we must enter the kingdom of God" (Acts 14:22).

Paul can therefore speak of the way believers will face a testing of fire before the day of final judgment. After talking about building on the foundation of Jesus Christ, he goes on to say,

> . . . each man's work will become manifest; for the Day will disclose it, because it will be revealed with fire, and the fire will test what sort of work each one has done. If the work which any man has built on the foundation survives, he will receive a reward. If any man's work is burned up, he will suffer loss, though he himself will be saved, but only as through fire. (1 Corinthians 3:10–15)

Salvation therefore includes having some of one's work "burned up." It means "suffering"—the believer will suffer loss. Salvation occurs "but only as through fire."

This is consistent with Jesus's teaching, "Everyone will be salted with fire" (Mark 9:49). As one Jewish scholar suggests, this passage seems to refer to being "preserved (from worse fate) by punishment that is short of destruction."[9] Or, as Protestant scholar Craig Evans explains the verse, "the one who submits to the purifying fire of Jesus will escape Gehenna."[10]

---

8     NRSV slightly adapted.
9     See, e.g., Lawrence M. Wills, "Mark," in *The Jewish Annotated New Testament*, 90.
10    Craig Evans, *Mark 8:27–16:20* (Nashville: Thomas Nelson, 2001), 73.

### Filling Up What Is Lacking for the Sake of the Body

Once again, however, we must be on guard against viewing salvation as occurring in an individualistic way. The New Testament presents salvation as occurring through believers' communion with one another. This is particularly true of suffering. Paul writes, "If one member suffers, all suffer together; if one member is honored, all rejoice together" (1 Corinthians 12:26).

What Christ has done in his personal body is now accomplished in his mystical body, the Church. Since Christ suffered redemptively for the sake of others in his personal body, the Church as his body now shares in this aspect of his work. The Apostle therefore writes, "*If we are afflicted, it is for your comfort and salvation. Our hope for you is unshaken; for we know that as you share in our sufferings, you will also share in our comfort*" (2 Corinthians 1:6–7). Because they are so closely united to one another, Christ's members share in one another's suffering. They also share together in the effects of one another's suffering.

The notion that believers share in Christ's work through suffering is more fully articulated in Colossians. There we read: "Now I rejoice in my sufferings for your sake, and in my flesh I complete what is lacking in Christ's afflictions for the sake of his body, that is, the church" (Colossians 1:24). As St. Thomas Aquinas explained, this should not be misinterpreted as indicating the heretical position that Christ's passion "was not sufficient for our redemption, and that the sufferings of the saints were added to complete it."[11] Instead, the passage indicates that Christ's body, the Church, must participate in the work of her head, Christ himself.

What is "lacking" according to Colossians 1 is not Christ's sufferings on the cross, but the Church's full participation in

---

11    *Commentary on Colossians*, no. 61.

his redemptive work. Each member contributes to the growth of the whole body by suffering. In this, believers actually suffer with Christ for others, that is, the other members. Paul can thus say in Colossians that his sufferings are "for your sake" (Colossians 1:24).

The Church suffers as a whole and offers up that suffering as one sacrifice in union with Christ. Paul therefore exhorts the church in Rome, saying, "present your *bodies* as a living *sacrifice*, holy and acceptable to God, which is your spiritual worship" (Romans 12:1). The Apostle instructs believers to offer their bodies (plural) as a "living sacrifice" (singular). The members offer themselves up in communion with one another as one offering. *Salvation is found in giving oneself away for others in union with Christ and his body.* Because of this, as we have seen, the Church is the body of Christ and is also a temple.

Through sharing in Christ's work, the Church "grows" into her head, Christ. This is what Ephesians envisions: ". . . you are fellow citizens with the saints and members of the household of God, built upon the foundation of the apostles and prophets, Christ Jesus himself being the cornerstone, in whom the whole structure is joined together and grows into a holy temple in the Lord" (Ephesians 2:19–21). Or, as 1 Peter suggests, believers are "built into" one another as a temple in which they are called to offer sacrifices to God.

> Come to him, to that living stone, rejected by men but in God's sight chosen and precious; and like living stones be yourselves built into a spiritual house, to be a holy priesthood, to offer spiritual sacrifices acceptable to God through Jesus Christ. (1 Peter 2:4–5)

The members of the Church offer their sacrifices together as one temple in Christ. By sacrificing themselves as *one,* they participate in Christ's work in communion with one another.

## PURGATORY AND SALVATION

Salvation involves growing in maturity. What happens, however, to a person who dies prior to being fully conformed to Christ? With this we come to the Catholic doctrine of purgatory. At first glance, this teaching may seem like a mere "add-on" to the biblical doctrine of salvation. But to view it in those terms is to misunderstand its significance. The Catholic teaching on purgatory is no addendum to the Gospel. Rather, purgatory actually *preserves* a key dimension of the New Testament's message, namely, that salvation involves nothing less than being "conformed" to Christ.

### *Becoming Perfect and the Prospect of Temporary Punishment*
As we have been stressing, salvation involves more than simply being forgiven. It entails sharing in Christ's own sonship. As Paul tells us, those in Christ are called "to be conformed to the image of [God's] son" (Romans 8:29). This is not hyperbole. In the Sermon on the Mount, Jesus describes the goal of Christian discipleship in no uncertain terms: "You, therefore, must be *perfect*, as your heavenly Father is perfect" (Matthew 5:48). This is a hard saying. Yet it should not be dismissed as a rhetorical exaggeration.

Though the standard of perfection seems unrealistically high, Jesus means what he says about it. As we have mentioned, the disciples later marvel when he tells the rich man what he must do in order to be "perfect." Jesus gives no indication that he is merely speaking hyperbolically. Rather, he responds, to their astonishment, "With men this is impossible, but *with God all things are possible*" (Matthew 19:26).

Jesus *is* asking for the impossible. On our own power, we cannot accomplish what he asks from us. We must not play this down or we will minimize our need for grace. Saving faith trusts that God's grace *can* make us like Christ. God's grace consists of Christ working within us. We can become like Christ because of Christ.

In the Sermon on the Mount, therefore, Jesus insists, "... unless your righteousness exceeds that of the scribes and Pharisees, you will never enter the kingdom of heaven" (Matthew 5:20). He elaborates on what this "surpassing righteousness" looks like in six sayings which quote or summarize Old Testament commandments. Jesus insists that these standards are in some way inadequate to express the righteousness required in the new covenant.[12] Here let us consider the first of these sayings:

> You have heard that it was said to the men of old, "You shall not kill; and whoever kills shall be liable to judgment." But I say to you that every one who is angry with his brother shall be liable to judgment; whoever insults his brother shall be liable to the council, and whoever says, "You fool!" shall be liable to the hell of fire. So if you are offering your gift at the altar, and there remember that your brother has something against you, leave your gift there before the altar and go; first be reconciled to your brother, and then come and offer your gift. Make friends quickly with your accuser, while you are going with him to court, lest your accuser hand you over to the judge, and the judge to the guard, and you be put in prison; truly, I say to you, you will never get out till you have paid the last penny. (Matthew 5:21–26)

A few observations about this passage are in order.

First, Jesus teaches that whoever merely says, "You fool!" will be liable to the "hell of fire" (Matthew 5:42). Some would like to dismiss this as an exaggeration, but that would be a mistake. As we have seen, Jesus insists that salvation entails being "perfect" (Matthew 5:48). To dismiss Jesus's teaching as hyperbole blunts its force. "Hell" seems to be a very real

---

12    For example, Jesus specifically overturns the Old Testament allowance for divorce and remarriage. See Michael Patrick Barber, "Jesus as the 'Fulfillment' of the Law and His Teaching on Divorce in Matthew," *Letter & Spirit* 9 (2014): 31–50.

possibility for those who insult others—after all, that is what Jesus's words actually mean.

Second, the lesson about settling with one's accuser before going to court is obviously related to the larger teaching, which, in context, refers to divine judgment. The judge is obviously an image for God. Being thrown into prison is therefore related to the notion of divine judgment.

Notice, however, that the saying appears to suggest that a *temporary* rather than *permanent* punishment is in view: ". . . you will never get out *until you have paid the last penny*" (Matthew 5:26). A similar idea seems to be found in Matthew 18, where Jesus describes a servant who, after being forgiven, refused to show mercy to a fellow servant. Jesus explains that this unmerciful servant received punishment: ". . . his lord delivered him to the jailers, *till he should pay all his debt*" (Matthew 18:34).

### Jewish and Christian Thought on Purification after Death

Many of the early Church Fathers believed these statements in Matthew 5 and 18 revealed that God's judgment would involve some sort of temporary punishment. For early writers such as St. Cyprian of Carthage (d. 258) and St. Ambrose of Milan (d. 397), this temporary judgment was linked to the notion that suffering in this life could bring about purification.[13] The context of the passage, however, would seem to point beyond such a reading. As we have seen, in Matthew 5, Jesus speaks of "hell."

Does Jesus really mean that those who say, "You fool!" will necessarily suffer eternal damnation? This seems unlikely. Notably, in the original Greek, Jesus speaks of "Gehenna." The word originally referred to the Valley of Hinnom (cf.

---

13    See, e.g., Cyprian, *Epistle* 55 [51], 20; Ambrose, *Exposition on Luke*, 7.1697–1709. For a detailed survey see Nathan Eubank, "Prison, Penance or Purgatory: The Interpretation of Matthew 5:25–26 and Its Parallels," *New Testament Studies* 64 (2018): 162–77.

Joshua 15:8; 18:6), in Aramaic, *gêhinnām*. This is an actual place, which lies just outside of Jerusalem. Writers often claim it served as a burning trash heap, but there is no evidence to support that idea. How then did it become associated with divine punishment?

In the Bible, the Valley of Hinnom is the place where wicked Israelites offered children as human sacrifices to pagan gods (2 Chronicles 28:3; 33:6). The prophets therefore issued frequent condemnations of the site.[14] In later Jewish literature it is identified as the place of God's final judgment and as the place where the wicked dead will be tormented.

While it often goes unnoticed, it is worth pointing out that in ancient Jewish sources Gehenna is not necessarily a place of *never-ending* punishment. The Mishnah, a second-century collection of rabbinic sayings, tells us that the renowned Rabbi Akiba taught that "*the judgment of the unrighteous in Gehenna shall endure twelve months.*"[15] Aware of such statements, the early twentieth-century scholar R. H. Charles observed that "Gehenna was regarded as the Purgatory of faithless Jews who were afterwards to be admitted into Paradise."[16]

Not surprisingly, then, some of the earliest Christian writers saw Jesus's reference to "paying the last penny" as indicating a purification of the righteous through suffering after death. Origen, who died around 254 AD, cited Matthew 18 in connection with the notion of being "purified by the fire of wisdom."[17] Gregory of Nyssa (d. 394) also writes,

> The just judgment of God extends to all, adjusting the intensity
> of the recompense depending on the weight of the debt, but

---

14    See Jeremiah 7:30–33; 19:1–13; 32:34–35; cf. also Isaiah 31:9; 66:24; 2 Kings 23:10; Leviticus 18:21.

15    Mishnah Eduyoth 2.10. See also the later statements in the Babylonian Talmud, Shabbat 33b and Rosh Hashanah 16b–17a.

16    R. H. Charles, *The Book of Enoch or 1 Enoch* (2d ed.; Oxford: Clarendon, 1912), 56.

17    Origen, *On the Lord's Prayer*, 29.15, translation from *Tertullian, Cyprian, and Origen on the Lord's Prayer* (New York: Crestwood, 2004), 201.

without overlooking even the smallest fault . . . When debtors have laid aside all that is alien to them—which is sin—and have stripped off the shame of their debts, they pass into freedom and confidence.[18]

For Gregory, the settling of accounts after death is not primarily punitive but restorative. God's mercy sees to it that no one remains with the "shame" of debts upon entering into glory.

As Nathan Eubank shows, no writer in the first three hundred years of Christianity seemed to think the sayings of Jesus in Matthew 5 and 18 referred to a permanent place of suffering.[19] As time went on, however, some became concerned that these passages could be used by heretics who rejected the idea of everlasting punishment altogether. Because of such concerns, the interpretations suggested by Origen and Gregory were muted.

Nevertheless, in light of the context, the most natural way to read Jesus's teaching in Matthew 5 is to see it as alluding to early Jewish views of a temporary place of punishment. Despite the fact that other teachings of Jesus describe Gehenna as a place of everlasting torment, there is no reason to think the word *always* refers to never-ending suffering. If other ancient Jews could envision a purgatorial Gehenna—that is, one from which release would inevitably occur—it makes sense to think that Matthew 5 could also view it in terms of a temporary punishment.

### A Holy and Pious Thought to Pray for the Dead

The ancient Jewish work known as 2 Maccabees, written around a hundred years before the birth of Jesus, contains a key passage that also points to the notion of some kind of postmortem purification. Although it is not found in most

---

18   *On the Soul and the Resurrection*, 15.75–6.
19   Eubank, "Prison, Penance or Purgatory," 172.

non-Catholic Bibles, 2 Maccabees was regarded as Scripture by most Christians prior to the Protestant Reformation in the sixteenth century. Yet even if one does not hold it to be a biblical book, it still offers a helpful backdrop for understanding ancient Jewish perspectives on the fate of the dead.

Second Maccabees recounts the miraculous victory of the Jews over a vicious Greek ruler, Antiochus Epiphanes, who ruthlessly persecutes the Jewish faith. A key figure in the story is Judas "Maccabeus" ("the Hammer"), who, inspired by zeal for God's law, leads an army that drives back the pagan oppressors. In the end, he rededicates the temple. The events in the book represent the origins of the Jewish feast of Hanukkah.

In the book, the unlikely success of Judas Maccabeus's army is chalked up to the people's faithfulness to God's law. A striking exception to this theme though is found in 2 Maccabees 12. There we read about a battle in which Judas's army suffers a devastating defeat. A shocking discovery is made when the bodies of the dead are examined: the fallen Jewish soldiers had been carrying trinkets connected to pagan idolatry, a clear violation of the Torah.

Judas's response to this development is remarkable. He takes up a collection so that sin offerings might be offered to God on behalf of the dead (2 Maccabees 12:43). We are told that Judas looked forward "to the splendid reward *that is laid up* for those who fall asleep in godliness" (2 Maccabees 12:45). On account of this, his action is called "a holy and pious thought" (2 Maccabees 12:45). Through his action, he "made atonement for the dead, *that they might be delivered from their sin*" (2 Maccabees 12:46).

The dead who are the subject of Judas's concerns are clearly not in heaven or in a place of eternal damnation. If either were the case, prayers on their behalf would be pointless. Yet the book does indicate that the prayers of the living can in some way help those who are deceased.

### *Purification, Catholic Tradition, and Purgatory*

The doctrine of purgatory was developed to preserve all of these biblical threads. It takes seriously (1) that salvation involves truly becoming perfect in Christ, (2) the teaching that suffering has purifying value, (3) Jesus's sayings that suggest the concept of a place of temporary punishment for sin, and (4) Paul's words about purification through fire. In short, purgatory explains how it is that purification or "purgation" can occur after death.

St. Augustine, for example, wrote:

> Now, we grant that even in this mortal life some punishments are purgatorial . . . they are purgatorial for those who are corrected and reformed under their constraints . . . As for temporal punishments, some suffer them only in this life, others after death, and still others both in this life and after death, but always prior to the final and most severe judgment. Nor does everyone who undergoes temporal punishments after death come under the eternal punishments which will follow that judgment. For, as we have already said, there are some for whom what is not forgiven in this world will be "forgiven in the world to come." [citing Matthew 12:32] [20]

The "punishments" for sin, therefore, are not simply punitive. They include a restorative dimension.

In light of the New Testament, however, we can go further. As we have seen, salvation in Christ is not merely understood individualistically. Those who are saved receive salvation through communion with Christ's body. The Church, then,

---

20    *City of God*, 22.13. Cited from *The City of God* (New York City: New City Press, 2013), 468.

grows *together*. The sufferings of those in Christ benefit the other members of the body.

According to the biblical authors, the mystical union believers have in Christ does not terminate in death. Romans 8 emphasizes that "nothing shall separate us from the love of Christ," including "death" (Romans 8:38–39). Likewise, in 1 Thessalonians we hear that "whether we wake or sleep we might live with him. Therefore encourage one another and build one another up, just as you are doing" (1 Thessalonians 5:10–11). Whether we "wake" (live in this world) or "sleep" (experience death), all Christians "live" in Christ. Catholic teaching therefore holds that the command to "build one another up" can even apply to those who already sleep in death.

In keeping with the Jewish piety exhibited with 2 Maccabees, early Christian sources talk about offering spiritual sacrifices and prayers to God on behalf of the dead. The early third-century account of the death of Perpetua and Felicity relates how Perpetua prays for her young brother, who was experiencing suffering in the afterlife: "I trusted that I could help him in his suffering. And I prayed for him every day . . ."[21] Later, she has a vision that assures her "that he was freed from his suffering."[22] In the fourth century, Cyril of Jerusalem speaks of how Christians pray for the souls of the dead during the celebration of the Eucharist: ". . . when we offer to [God] our supplications *for those who have fallen asleep*, though they be sinners . . . offer up Christ sacrificed for our sins, *propitiating our merciful God for them as well as for ourselves*."[23] Likewise, St. Monica, St. Augustine's mother, told him prior to his death: "Lay this body anywhere, and take

---

21    *The Passion of Perpetua and Felicity* 7.9. Translation from Thomas J. Heffernan, *The Passion of Perpetua and Felicity* (Oxford: Oxford University Press, 2012), 129.

22    Ibid., 8.4.

23    Cyril of Jerusalem, *Catechetical Lectures*, 10.

no trouble over it. One thing only do I ask of you, that you remember me at the altar of the Lord wherever you may be."[24]

Salvation involves more than simply getting out of hell—it is found in being fully conformed to Christ. If we view salvation solely as the moment one receives forgiveness of sins, we can easily fall into the trap of minimizing the need for spiritual maturity. Recognizing that salvation is sharing in Christ's own sonship is essential to avoiding a reductive understanding of what believers are saved *for*—being conformed to the image of God's Son. Becoming "perfect" is not a mere ideal—it is the fullest meaning of salvation.

If we fail to emphasize the need to be fully conformed to Christ, suffering appears meaningless. Why would a merciful God allow us to experience pain and humiliation in this life? While the specific reasons remain a mystery, in times of darkness one thing is important to recall: the New Testament maintains that Christ's own humanity was perfected by suffering. Suffering is not an indication that God has abandoned his people or that he is powerless in the face of evil. On the contrary, God permits suffering because, by virtue of his wisdom and power, he can use it to save the world. We learn that through suffering with Christ we can participate in the redemption of the whole body.

Purgatory is no mere supplement to the doctrine of salvation. Belief in purgatory upholds perfection—conformity to Christ—as the true goal of salvation. It also upholds the communal dimension of salvation; not even death can separate us from the bond we have together in Christ. To be in Christ, therefore, is to suffer with him and to offer ourselves *for* others through union with him.

---

24  Augustine, *Confessions*, 9.11.27 cited from *The Confessions* (Hyde Park: New City Press, 1997), 230.

As we have seen, Scripture does speak of temporary punishment. But in addition to that, the biblical writers also speak of an even greater evil: everlasting punishment. In the next chapter we will consider this aspect of the New Testament's teaching.

## 8

# Not Inevitable

On that day many will say to me, "Lord, Lord, did we not prophesy in your name, and cast out demons in your name, and do many mighty works in your name?" And then will I declare to them, "I never knew you; depart from me, you evildoers."

—Matthew 5:22–23

Those who pray are certainly saved; those who do not pray are certainly damned.

—St. Alphonsus Liguori
cited in *Catechism of the Catholic Church* §2744

When I was a teenager, I enrolled in classes at a Catholic parish that would prepare me to receive the sacrament of Confirmation. The first session took me by surprise. The teacher opened by explaining that the Catholic Church had made some recent changes to its official teaching. He named one specific doctrine the Church had nixed: hell.

Not long after this, the *Catechism of the Catholic Church* was published in English. I suspect my confirmation instructor was astonished to discover that it reaffirms the reality of hell. Quoting from the Second Vatican Council, it affirms, "Following the example of Christ, the Church warns the faithful of the 'sad and lamentable reality of eternal death' also called 'hell'" (§1056). The existence of hell has been reiterated more recently by both Pope Benedict XVI and Pope Francis. That said, hell is often misunderstood.

In fact, in this book I have been deliberately delaying a discussion about the topic of hell. I have been emphasizing the point that salvation entails much more than merely avoiding divine punishment. I have wanted to highlight that it is becoming united to God through incorporation into Christ and his body. My hope is that readers will recognize that salvation relates to this present life and is not just a distant future reality.

Nevertheless, we cannot ignore the New Testament's teaching about hell altogether. As we shall see, without hell we run the risk of misunderstanding salvation in the New Testament. Like purgatory, the doctrine of hell actually preserves a key dimension of the biblical doctrine of salvation in Christ.

In this chapter, we will look at three key dimensions of the New Testament's teaching that relate to damnation. First, the New Testament authors indicate that, in the end, not all will be saved; there is a place of everlasting punishment for the wicked. Second, we shall see that it is possible for a person who once was united to Christ to be severed from him and end up among the damned. Third and finally, the biblical authors indicate that those who fail to attain salvation have only themselves to blame; those who end up there do so because of their own choices.

## "FOR MANY WILL SEEK TO ENTER AND WILL NOT BE ABLE"

If there is one topic relating to salvation that we would rather avoid it would have to be hell. Yet we simply cannot dodge the issue. The doctrine of hell is a very real part of the New

Testament's message. This sections offers a brief overview of some key passages that describe it.

### Unquenchable Fire

Though the New Testament indicates that God "desires all men to be saved" (1 Timothy 2:4), numerous passages indicate that not all will be. Let us return here to a passage we have already examined, Jesus's description of the final judgment in Matthew 25. As we have seen, in this passage Jesus promises that the righteous will be given admittance into the kingdom. They will discover that whatever they did for "the least of these my brethren" they also did to him (Matthew 25:40). Yet Jesus goes on to make another point: there will be individuals who are not be saved.

The judgment scene begins with a "separation" of the righteous and the wicked:

> When the Son of man comes in his glory, and all the angels with him, then he will sit on his glorious throne. Before him will be gathered all the nations, and he will separate them one from another as a shepherd separates the sheep from the goats, and he will place the sheep at his right hand, but the goats at the left. (Matthew 25:31–33)

Jesus tells us that the sheep—those on the right—will enter the kingdom. Yet we also read about what will happen to those on the left, namely, those who failed to show compassion to the hungry, the thirsty, the sick, etc. Jesus says that he will say to them, "Depart from me, you cursed, into the eternal fire prepared for the devil and his angels" (Matthew 25:41). These, Jesus declares, are those who will "go away into eternal punishment" (Matthew 25:46).

Something similar is found in the book of Revelation: "The devil who had deceived them was thrown into the lake of fire and sulphur where the beast and the false prophet were, and *they will be tormented day and night for ever and ever*" (Revelation 20:10). The beast and the false prophet are symbols of human figures, not demons. This is not a "possible" future. John tells us that his visions involve things "that must take place" (Revelation 4:1).

Another passage worth considering appears in Jesus's famous Sermon on the Mount:

> Not every one who says to me, "Lord, Lord," shall enter the kingdom of heaven, but he who does the will of my Father who is in heaven. On that day many will say to me, "Lord, Lord, did we not prophesy in your name, and cast out demons in your name, and do many mighty works in your name?" And then will I declare to them, "I never knew you; depart from me, you evildoers." (Matthew 7:21–23)

There is, perhaps, no account of the day of judgment more chilling than this one. On the last day, there will be "many" who think they will be saved but who will not be. Despite invoking his name, performing great works, and even calling to him, "Lord, Lord," they will be turned away. Again, there is no indication that Jesus is talking about something that just *might* happen. Here Jesus speaks of an event that *will* take place.

Luke 13 contains a related teaching. There we read that Jesus was asked, "Lord, will those who are saved be few?" (Luke 13:23). Jesus's words are sobering: "Strive to enter by the narrow door; *for many, I tell you, will seek to enter and will not be able*" (Luke 13:24).

There are various passages in the New Testament that speak of God's universal desire to save. We have already quoted 1 Timothy 2:4: "God desires all men to be saved." Another expression of this is found in Romans: "Then as one man's trespass led to condemnation for all men, so one man's act of righteousness leads to acquittal and life *for all men*" (Romans

5:18). From this some have adduced that it may be possible to "hope" that, in the end, "all" will somehow be saved.[1]

This is a difficult position to insist on. It would mean that Jesus's announcements of what will take place at the end of time are unreliable or somehow only threats that he knows are ultimately empty. As others have shown, neither of these options is persuasive.[2] As uncomfortable as it makes us, according to the New Testament, hell is not only a real place, Jesus also announces that it will not go unpopulated. Moreover, it is worth noting that Jesus indicates that "many" are on their way there (cf. Luke 13:24).

Jesus's statement that it would have been better for Judas "if he had not been born" (Mark 14:21) is especially difficult to explain if he in fact ended up in heaven. What else could the line possibly mean? Doctors of the Church like Augustine and Aquinas took it, therefore, as a revealed truth that Judas ended up in hell.[3]

With this in mind, the Second Vatican Council exhorts us to be vigilant so that we do not become like "the wicked and slothful" in Jesus's teachings who are "ordered to depart into the eternal fire, into the outer darkness where 'men will weep and gnash their teeth.'"[4] Likewise, the *Catechism* explains, "The teaching of the Church affirms the existence of hell and its eternity" (§1035). In keeping with all of this, in 2014, Pope Francis exhorted those involved with the mafia with these words: "Convert, there is still time, *so that you don't end up in hell. That is what awaits you if you continue on this path.*"[5]

---

1 This position is most famously associated with Hans Urs von Balthasar, *Dare We Hope "That All Men Be Saved"?* (San Francisco: Ignatius Press, 1988 [1986]).

2 For thoughtful critiques of Balthasar's reading, see Germain Grisez and Peter F. Ryan, S.J., "Hell and Hope for Salvation," *New Blackfriars* 95 (2014): 606–614; Martin, *Will Many Be Saved?*, 129–90.

3 See, e.g., Augustine, *City of God*, 1.17; Aquinas, *On Truth*, q. 6, art. 2, ad. 11.

4 Vatican II, *Lumen Gentium*, 48 §3.

5 Francis, Address at the Prayer Vigil for the Nineteenth "Memorial and Commitment Day" (March 21, 2014).

### Ongoing Punishment

Some have attempted to downplay the imagery the New Testament uses for hell by highlighting the way it is culturally shaped. After all, hell is associated with a particular location, the Valley of Hinnom. Yet the fact that damnation is described with imagery from a particular time and place does not somehow call the notion of the reality of eternal punishment into question.

It is necessary to emphasize that, according to Jesus, hell involves something more than merely spiritual punishment. In the Gospel of Matthew, Jesus explains, "And do not fear those who kill the body but cannot kill the soul; rather fear him who can destroy both soul and body in hell" (Matthew 10:28). Damnation includes a *physical* dimension. It affects not only the soul but the whole human person, that is, it includes the body. This is also hinted at in the Gospel according to John. Jesus states,

> . . . the hour is coming when all who are in the tombs will hear his voice and come forth, those who have done good, to the resurrection of life, and those who have done evil, to the resurrection of judgment. (John 5:28–29)

Following from this, Christian tradition has long held that *all* will get their bodies back on the last day. The righteous will experience salvation in an embodied way, but the damned also get their bodies back. According to fathers and doctors of the Church such as Augustine and Aquinas, the sufferings of those in hell will not merely be spiritual or mental, but, as Scripture indicates, will also include *physical* pain.[6]

Moreover, despite the claims of groups such as Jehovah's Witnesses, the New Testament indicates that the suffering of the damned will be *ongoing.* Hell is not simply "annihilation"

---

6    See, e.g., Augustine, *City of God*, 21.9; Aquinas, *Summa Contra Gentiles*, IV, 88–89.

but involves unending affliction. In the Apocalypse, we read that *"the smoke of their torment goes up for ever and ever;* and *they have no rest, day or night"* (Revelation 14:11). Later in the same book, damnation is described in terms of a lake of fire where the wicked *"will be tormented day and night for ever and ever"* (Revelation 20:10). As noted above, Jesus speaks of hell in terms of "eternal fire" (Matthew 25:41) and "eternal punishment" (Matthew 25:46).

Some have argued that the Greek for "eternal" (*aiōnios*) need not be interpreted as referring to never-ending suffering. This is difficult to maintain. In John, Jesus uses the same Greek term to refer to "eternal life," which should not be viewed as a temporary reality. The extended nature of the suffering of hell is also emphasized in other ways. Jesus refers to it as the place where "their worm does not die, and the fire is not quenched" (Mark 9:48). The saying here is drawn from Isaiah 66:24, a passage which is very difficult to interpret as relating the idea of "temporary" punishment of the wicked.

Jesus also links damnation to sorrow: ". . . men will weep and gnash their teeth" (Matthew 8:12). The language here coheres with what we find elsewhere. Salvation is associated with happiness and joy. It only makes sense, then, that hell would involve sorrow and bitterness.

Before moving on, it is worth noting that Paul himself is explicit that certain sins disqualify one from the kingdom of God. In 1 Corinthians, Paul warns: ". . . neither the immoral, nor idolaters, nor adulterers, nor sexual perverts, nor thieves, nor the greedy, nor drunkards, nor revilers, nor robbers *will inherit the kingdom of God"* (1 Corinthians 6:9–10). In other words, there are sins that actually bar a person from salvation if one fails to repent of them (cf. Galatians 5:19–21).

## MORTAL SIN AND SEVERING ONESELF FROM CHRIST

For many Christians, once one receives salvation, it can never be lost. Catholic teaching does not accept this view. According to the New Testament, God will not coerce anyone to be saved against his or her will. A person who is united to Christ can choose to be separated from him. This spotlights an important feature of the Gospel message: God gives us the ability to choose him or reject him.

### *Eternal Security in Paul?*

"Once saved, always saved" is a principle preached from many a pulpit. This view, also referred to as "eternal security," aims to preserve the idea that salvation is by God's grace. Since salvation is due to God's gift, it is thought that one's salvation cannot be jeopardized by committing sin. Advocates of "eternal security" insist that because Christ saves us by *his* righteousness and not our own, nothing we do can cause us to lose our salvation.

The classic biblical passage cited in support of eternal security is found in Romans 8. Here Paul indicates that nothing can separate believers from Christ:

> For I am sure that neither death, nor life, nor angels, nor principalities, nor things present, nor things to come, nor powers, nor height, nor depth, nor anything else in all creation, will be able to separate us from the love of God in Christ Jesus our Lord. (Romans 8:38–39)

What is often overlooked, however, is this: Paul does not mention *sin* in this context. The Apostle's point is not that believers do not possess the ability to reject their union with Christ. In context, he is talking about persecution. Look at the preceding verses:

Who shall separate us from the love of Christ? Shall tribulation, or distress, or persecution, or famine, or nakedness, or peril, or sword? As it is written, "For thy sake we are being killed all the day long; we are regarded as sheep to be slaughtered" [Psalm 44:22]. No, in all these things we are more than conquerors through him who loved us. (Romans 8:35–37).

It is wrong to read Romans 8:38–39 as endorsing "eternal security." To insist that these verses reject the notion that believers can cut themselves off from Christ is to wrench Paul's teaching out of context. Paul is *not* denying the idea that believers can separate themselves from Christ by sin.

Some might suggest eternal security is implied in Paul's teaching that "those whom he predestined he also called; and those whom he called he also justified; and those whom he justified he also glorified" (Romans 8:30). Yet Paul does *not* say that God *only* justifies those who are predestined to glory. Some could experience salvation and yet not be one who "endures to the end" (Mark 13:13). In such cases, they would have been saved momentarily but not been among those "predestined." These would not be the "elect," that is, those who have been "given" to Jesus who are promised to persevere (cf. John 6:39).

Paul talks as if losing salvation is in fact a real possibility for him: "I pommel my body and subdue it, *lest after preaching to others I myself should be disqualified*" (1 Corinthians 9:27). Later in the same epistle he tells believers: "Now I would remind you, brethren, in what terms I preached to you the gospel, which you received, in which you stand, by which you are saved, if you hold it fast—*unless you believed in vain*" (1 Corinthians 15:1–2). Again, the natural reading of Paul's words is that salvation is not necessarily automatic; believers must "hold fast" to the Gospel to be saved. This seems to have been Jesus's teaching: "He who endures to the end will be saved" (Mark 13:13).

In 1 Corinthians 4 we find a passage that makes it especially difficult to think Paul believed he was "assured" of salvation.

> But with me it is a very small thing that I should be judged by you or by any human court. I do not even judge myself. I am not aware of anything against myself, but I am not thereby acquitted. It is the Lord who judges me. Therefore do not pronounce judgment before the time, before the Lord comes, who will bring to light the things now hidden in darkness and will disclose the purposes of the heart. Then every man will receive his commendation from God. (1 Corinthians 4:3–5)

Despite attempts to make him say otherwise, the Apostle is quite clear: no one should "pronounce judgment" before the day of the Lord.

### Being Severed from Christ

Moreover, in other places in his letters Paul explicitly insists that believers can separate themselves from Christ. For example, in his letter to the Galatians, Paul writes to Gentile believers who are being told by some that they must be circumcised to be saved. Circumcision was a visible sign in the Old Testament of belonging to the people of God. Its importance in the Old Testament is clear. One can easily see why Gentiles may have felt persuaded that they should undergo the rite.

Paul, however, stresses that one should not put confidence in the flesh, but in faith in Christ. He warns Gentile believers that if they give into these pressures and become convinced that faith is insufficient, they put their salvation at risk. He warns that if they do this: "*You are severed from Christ . . . you have fallen away from grace*" (Galatians 5:4).

A similar image is found in Romans 11. In this chapter, Paul compares Gentile members of the community to "wild olive branches" that have been "grafted" into the "tree" of Israel. In particular, the Apostle warns that Gentile believers can be "cut off" if they do not remain faithful. He reminds them of God's kindness towards them, which will be theirs, "provided you continue in his kindness; otherwise *you too will be cut off*" (Romans 11:22).

Other New Testament books also affirm the possibility of being cut off from Christ. For example, in the Gospel according to John, Jesus indicates that some who were once "in him" will face the fires of damnation. Specifically, he talks about the importance of "abiding" or "remaining" in him, warning that some who at one point were "in him" will be cut off and cast into fire:

> I am the vine, you are the branches. *He who abides in me, and I in him, he it is that bears much fruit*, for apart from me you can do nothing. If a man does not abide in me, *he is cast forth as a branch and withers*; and the branches are gathered, *thrown into the fire and burned*. (John 15:5–6)

Attempts to make this passage cohere with eternal security are unpersuasive. For example, the sixteenth-century Protestant Reformer John Calvin thought that the branches that are burned symbolize those who only "appear" to have been Christians.[7] A more recent suggestion is that the language of burning refers to *temporary judgment,* that is, purifying trials.

These are not persuasive readings. As one non-Catholic writer observes, "Jesus does not say, 'those who appear to be in me' but every branch *in me*."[8] Likewise, the context makes clear that Jesus does not speak here of purifying suffering. Why would a vinedresser cut off and "burn" a branch in order to restore it?

The teaching in John 15 makes it difficult to maintain that Jesus's teaching elsewhere in the same Gospel suggests

---

7    John Calvin, *The Gospel According to St. John: Part Two, 11–21 and the First Epistle of John* (Grand Rapids: Eerdmans, 1959).
8    Rodney A. Whitacre, *John* (Downers Grove: InterVarsity Press, 1999), 373–374.

believers can never lose their salvation. A favorite passage in this regard is John 10: "My sheep hear my voice . . . and I give them eternal life, and they shall never perish, and no one shall snatch them out of my hand" (John 10:28). Again, Jesus's point here is that believers will not be separated from Christ by *others*. Yet John 15 shows us that it is possible for one to be severed from Christ.

### Mortal Sin and Apostasy

It is possible, then, for those who have been united to Christ to separate themselves from him. If humans can accept God's gift by a choice, they can also choose to turn away from it—to commit the sin of "apostasy." The letter to the Hebrews is particularly adamant about this:

> *For it is impossible to restore again to repentance those who have once been enlightened,* who have tasted the heavenly gift, and have become partakers of the Holy Spirit . . . *if they then commit apostasy* . . . (Hebrews 6:4, 6; cf. Hebrews 10:26)

Here the author specifically has in view those who have received the "heavenly gift," which would seem to be a reference to membership in the new covenant. The point is not that *any* sin whatsoever makes repentance impossible. The author is referring to "apostasy," which is presented as "continuous" or "ongoing" rejection of Christ. Such a person is like "thorns and thistles," whose *"end is to be burned"* (Hebrew 6:8).

There are some sins, then, that can sever one's relationship with Christ. A similar idea is found in 1 John. There we read that not all sins are equal in gravity; there are some that are "mortal" or "deadly."

> If any one sees his brother committing what is not a mortal sin, he will ask, and God will give him life for those whose sin is not mortal. There is sin which is mortal; I do not say that one is to

pray for that. All wrongdoing is sin, but there is sin which is not mortal. (1 John 5:16–17)

"Mortal" sin is that which causes spiritual death. While believers' prayers for one another can strengthen one another, some sins are so serious they require something more for restoration.

To preserve this aspect of the New Testament's teaching, Catholic tradition distinguishes between "mortal" and "venial" sin. Mortal sin cuts the believer off from Christ and his body. For a sin to be "mortal" it must fulfill certain requirements. It must involve grave matter, it must be committed with full knowledge, and it must be committed with deliberate consent (*Catechism* §1857). That said, even venial sin represents a danger to one's spiritual life. It offends God's love, weakens one's ability to resist temptation, and disposes us to be more inclined to commit mortal sins (*Catechism* §1862–63).

In Catholic teaching, restoration from mortal sin is found in the sacrament of Penance (also known as sacramental "confession") or by an act perfect contrition which includes the intention to go to confession (*Catechism* §1452). As we mentioned above, the notion of confessing sins to another is found in James 5. Of course, regular confession of venial sin is also strongly encouraged since, among other things, through the sacrament grace is imparted, which helps us overcome it (*Catechism* §1496).

## TAKING ONESELF TO HELL

For many, hell poses the ultimate contradiction. How can eternal torment be reconciled with Scripture's teaching that "God is love" (1 John 4:8)? It seems impossible to believe that the Lord would consign those whom he dearly loves to the fires of eternal torment. Yet Scripture teaches that those in hell take themselves there.

### Sin as a Human Choice

Various passages in the Old Testament affirm that humans have the ability to choose to obey or disobey God's commandments.

> I have set before you life and death, blessing and curse; therefore choose life . . . (Deuteronomy 30:19)

> *These [sinners] have chosen their own ways* . . . when I called, no one answered, when I spoke they did not listen; but they did what was evil in my eyes, and *chose that in which I did not delight.* (Isaiah 66:3, 4)

> If you will, you can keep the commandments, and to act faithfully is *a matter of your own choice.* (Sirach 15:15)

Of course, as we have seen, those who choose to be faithful do so with the help of grace. Nonetheless, no one is coerced to do evil.

To be sure, some attempt to make the case that God overrides human decision-making. For example, some point out that Exodus indicates that it was God who hardened Pharaoh's heart (e.g., Exodus 4:21; 7:3; 9:12; 10:1; 10:27). But to use this passage as proof that God cancels out free choice ignores the larger context of the book. On numerous occasions we learn that Pharaoh hardened his *own* heart (e.g., Exodus 7:13, 14, 22; 8:15, 19, 32; 9:7, 34, 35; 13:15). To claim God simply compelled Pharaoh to sin ignores these verses.

Some will also point to passages that emphasize the notion of predestination as proof that God predestines some to fall into sin. Along these lines, many have turned to Romans 9:

> You will say to me then, "Why does he still find fault? For who can resist his will?" But who are you, a man, to answer back to God? Will what is molded say to its molder, "Why have you made me thus?" Has the potter no right over the clay, to make out of the same lump one vessel for beauty and another for menial use? (Romans 9:19–21)

This passage should not be taken as indicating that God causes humans to sin against their will. Nor should it be read as suggesting that there are some who have no real choice but must do evil. Yes, Paul says the vessel should not reject the potter's designs. But, in context, Paul is *not* arguing that God forces some to be damned. Rather, Paul is actually making the *opposite* point. Here he insists that those who appear to be destined for destruction actually end up receiving mercy. A look at the Old Testament background of this passage confirms this reading.

Paul's teaching in Romans 9 quotes from Isaiah 29, which concludes, ". . . those who err in spirit *will come to understanding*, and *those who murmur will accept instruction*" (Isaiah 29:24). In other places, the prophets use the imagery of the potter and vessel to talk about the absurdity of questioning God's *mercy*. For example, in Jeremiah 18, the metaphor of God as potter is followed by the promise that if any nation God has threatened with destruction "turns from its evil," the Lord will not carry out his judgment (Jeremiah 18:10). To suggest that Paul is drawing from these passages to prove humans have no choice concerning their behavior is to ignore their overall message.

On the contrary, as we have seen, the New Testament urges people to repent of their sins, indicating that, as in the Old Testament, a choice has been set before them. To give merely one illustration, in the book of Revelation, Jesus exhorts the church in Ephesus with these words:

> I have this against you, that you have abandoned the love you had at first. Remember then from what you have fallen, repent and do the works you did at first. If not, I will come to you and remove your lampstand from its place, unless you repent. (Revelation 2:3–5)

Are we to assume that those who heard this actually had no choice over their behavior? Such a conclusion would obviously make little sense of Jesus's words.

The biblical authors do not teach that humans are coerced to do evil. Nevertheless, it would be misleading to say that the Bible teaches that humans have "freedom to sin." Scripture does not portray choosing evil as freedom. For authors such as Paul, true freedom is found in Christ.

Perhaps the best way to explain Scripture's teaching is to put it as follows: humans have the option to disobey. The Bible tells us that some do choose evil. The reason sin is a reality is because humans have the ability to make their own decisions.

### Hell as a Human Choice

Since God does not force us to choose him, he also does not coerce us to be united to him. For Paul, eternal judgment is "exclusion from the presence of the Lord" (2 Thessalonians 1:9). As we have seen, heaven is communion with God. Conversely, as the *Catechism* teaches, hell is separation from God (§1033).

The pain of hell is ghastly and unending. Nevertheless, let us remember, those who are in hell take themselves there by their own choices. The famous Christian writer C. S. Lewis describes hell as being "locked from the inside."[9]

How can this be? Who would willingly choose eternal torment? Well, according to Scripture, many. The idea should not be altogether unbelievable. Even in this life there is plenty of evidence that people do in fact make decisions they know are bad for them. With full knowledge that their behavior will lead to misery, people nevertheless persist in self-destructive conduct.

Why do many enter through the gate that goes to hell? Jesus tells us that choosing the way of life is hard: ". . . the

---

9    C. S. Lewis, *The Problem of Pain* (New York: Simon and Schuster, 1996 [1940]), 127.

gate is wide and the way is easy, that leads to destruction, and those who enter by it are many. For the gate is narrow and the way is hard, that leads to life, and those who find it are few" (Matthew 7:13–14). As we have seen, without God's help, doing what God asks of us is impossible.

The cross shows us just how much God asks of us; salvation involves nothing less than self-emptying. This is painful and involves making difficult choices. We can succeed, but only by God's grace. Those in hell are there because they refuse to give themselves away in love. They also refuse to trust in God's ability to make them righteous. They therefore isolate themselves from him. One Catholic priest described the attitude of the damned this way: "I don't want to love. I don't want to be loved. Just leave me to myself."[10]

### *I Never Knew You*

In the Sermon on the Mount, Jesus announces,

> On that day many will say to me, "Lord, Lord, did we not prophesy in your name, and cast out demons in your name, and do many mighty works in your name?" And then will I declare to them, "I never knew you; depart from me, you evildoers." (Matthew 7:22–23)

The ultimate criterion of salvation is *knowing the Lord*. With this in mind, we return to an idea we looked at earlier when we examined Jeremiah's new covenant prophecy: to be saved means to enter into an intimate relationship with God himself. This communion is inseparable from prayer.

The *Catechism* highlights Moses as a model for prayer. In particular, it highlights the way Scripture portrays the manner in which he "converses with God *often* and at *length*"

---

10    Fr. Herbert Alphonso cited by Regis Martin, *The Last Things* (San Francisco: Ignatius Press, 1998), 87.

(*Catechism* §2576). Both descriptors are important. Without speaking to one another "often," our relationships become weak. When we fail to speak to a friend with regularity, we inevitably "lose touch" and "drift apart."

Yet meaningful relationships entail more than frequent conversations. We can talk on a daily basis to the postal worker who delivers our mail, a person we see regularly in our neighborhood, or a coworker. These relationships can be cordial, but not necessarily close or intimate. To establish a truly deep bond of friendship with someone, we must enter into something more than regular "small talk." We must also talk "at length" with them about who we are and what we care about most. This entails a dialogue in which we not only talk but also listen.

How is it possible to have this kind of conversation with God? The Church teaches: "In the sacred books [of the Bible], *the Father who is in heaven comes lovingly to meet his children, and talks with them.*"[11] Catholic tradition recognizes that we hear God's Word in Sacred Scripture. Quoting St. Ambrose, the Catechism explains, ". . . prayer should accompany the reading of Sacred Scripture, so that a dialogue takes place between God and man. For '*we speak to him when we pray; we listen to him when we read the divine oracles*'" (§2653).

This involves more than simply passing our eyes over the pages of Scripture. To hear God speaking to us, we must do something more intentional than casually glance at the Bible's pages. Catholic teaching emphasizes the need for *meditation*, that is, the slow and thoughtful reading of Scripture. We can truly enter into a meaningful conversation with God wherein we are not simply *speaking* to him but *listening* to him by contemplating Sacred Scripture.

---

11   *Dei Verbum*, no. 21.

In this we can unite ourselves to Christ and, with his help, avoid becoming those who hear the dreadful words on the last day: "I never knew you." With all of this in mind, we can understand a disturbing quote from the *Catechism*, taken from St. Alphonsus Liguori: "Those who pray are certainly saved; those who do not pray are certainly damned (*Catechism* §2744).

As we saw above, this does not mean that salvation is necessarily impossible for non-Christians. It also does not mean that salvation is automatically guaranteed to all who do pray. Nevertheless, St. Alphonsus's teaching should challenge us to make prayer a priority. In our hectic lives, it is always easy to find other things to do instead of prayer. This is a temptation we must resist. Without prayer we will only separate ourselves from Christ, who invites us to know him.

And, indeed, contrary to the false security some may wish to impart, eternal separation from God *is a real possibility*. It is due to one thing above all: sin. The problem is, as we shall see in the next chapter, we often have trouble recognizing its presence in our own lives.

# 9

# Not Just for Other People

Why do you see the speck that is in your brother's eye, but do not notice the log that is in your own eye? . . . You hypocrite, *first take the log out of your own eye* . . .
—Matthew 7:3, 5

. . . since sin is universal, those who pretend not to need salvation are blind to themselves.
—*Catechism of the Catholic Church* §588

When I was a student at Azusa Pacific University, I was one of only a few Catholics on campus. My experience there was overwhelmingly positive. Nevertheless, there was one feature of student life that I sometimes found uncomfortable: chapel service.

To be fair, attending chapel was usually a good experience. The music was outstanding and most of the sermons were thought provoking. Still, every now and then a preacher would show up with a thinly-veiled anti-Catholic message. As you can imagine, these services were awkward for me.

One day, I was particularly bitter about having to be there. I cannot remember why. It may have been because I knew who the scheduled preacher was and anticipated hearing a frustrating sermon. It could have just been that I had woken up on the wrong side of the bed that day. Either way, I was on edge. I was sitting by myself when a female student came by and, motioning to the empty chair next to me, asked politely, "Is that seat saved?"

I looked up and said, "I don't know, let me ask." I then turned, looked at the empty chair, and said to it, "So, have you made Jesus your personal Lord and Savior?" The young woman was clearly not amused and walked away with a disgusted look on her face. It was not my proudest moment.

At the time, I thought I was being funny. Yet there was more to it than that. By making a joke about the seat being "saved," I was singling out a term that, for me, encapsulated the *non-Catholic* character of Azusa Pacific's chapel service. To my Catholic sensibilities, the language of being "saved" reflected a peculiarly *Protestant* preoccupation. My joke was an attempt—passive-aggressive and inappropriate as it was— to signal my discomfort with the approach to Christianity the preacher would likely offer.

Yet my attitude was uninformed. Why should a Catholic feel uncomfortable with the notion of being "saved"? As mentioned above, Catholics affirm the need for salvation. We specifically refer to Jesus as not only "the Lord" but also as "*the Savior.*" As we have said above, Jesus's name means "the Lord saves." Joseph is told, ". . . *you shall call his name Jesus*, for he will *save* his people from their sins" (Matthew 1:21). Jesus's name sums up the whole meaning of the biblical story—God sent his Son to save us from sin.

If we are being totally honest, I think we Catholics will admit that we prefer to speak of salvation in general rather than personal terms. Talking about Jesus as "the Lord" and "the Savior" is not strange to us. What sounds *un-Catholic* to our ears is referring to Jesus as "*my* Lord and Savior." Why that should be the case is a bit mystifying. In Luke's Gospel, Mary herself speaks of God as "*my* Savior" (Luke 1:47). Are Catholics uncomfortable with talking like the Virgin Mary does?

The reason we avoid talking about salvation should be fairly obvious: we do not like being reminded that *we* need saving. We are fine with the notion that Jesus is *the* Savior. We are content to affirm that he has come to bring salvation to the *world*.

But do *I* need to be saved? That is another thing altogether. To speak that way means admitting that *I* might be in danger. It reminds us that we are under a threat—and that is uncomfortable to think about.

When the angel appears to Joseph in a dream, the carpenter learns *why* God's people need a Savior: ". . . *he will save his people from their sins*" (Matthew 1:21). Notice that nothing at all is said here about hell. There is nothing mentioned about eternal punishment, a lake of fire, unending torment—those things are mentioned later, but not here. This should not go unnoticed. The truth is, in the New Testament, salvation is not simply about "spiritual fire insurance." Before anything else, the New Testament teaches us that Jesus comes to save us *from sin*.

Why is it that we do not like to talk much about *salvation*? I think, in part, it is because salvation leads us to the topic of sin. We do not like to think of ourselves as sinners. We tend to think we are doing just fine; *we* do not need to be saved. Salvation is for the "world," that is, for *others*. We do not like to think about *my* need for salvation.

In the Gospels, Jesus regularly encounters people with this outlook. He has a name for it: blindness.

## YOU ARE SPIRITUALLY BLIND . . . YES, *YOU!*

Most people today would rather not be called a "Pharisee." To be "Pharisaical" is to be self-righteous, smug, and hypocritical. While it is true that Jesus does condemn Pharisees who oppose him for these types of vices, it would be a mistake to view this

Jewish group as nothing more than one-dimensional villains. Recognizing that modern biblical scholarship has sometimes been shaped by anti-Semitic tendencies, commentators today insist on the need to pay closer attention to the nuances of our sources' depiction of these Jewish opponents of Jesus.[1] In fact, many in Jesus's day would have considered it a compliment to be known as a "Pharisee."

### *The Popularity of the Pharisees*

Our historical knowledge about the Pharisees is limited. Their name seems to be derived from the Aramaic word for "separatists" (plural *parishaya*). In all probability, the term became associated with them because they had a reputation for being zealous about "purity"; they would "separate" from anything they saw as "impure." To this end, they were devoted to maintaining traditions that sought to preserve their purity and ensure faithfulness to God's law (cf. Matthew 15:2; Mark 7:5; cf. Galatians 1:13).

Contrary to their reputation today, the Pharisees were not necessarily always strict or harsh. In the Gospels we learn that Jesus took a compassionate position when it came to saving an endangered animal on the Sabbath. Some Jews, like those who wrote the Dead Sea Scrolls, prohibited undertaking a rescue attempt.[2] Yet the Pharisees apparently agreed with Jesus that it was permissible to rescue an animal on the Sabbath. For Jesus, this makes their opposition to his healing on the Sabbath all the more frustrating. Jesus asks, "Which of you, having a son or an ox that has fallen into a well, will not immediately pull him out on a sabbath day?" (Luke 14:5; cf. Mark 12:12–13). Jesus puts the Pharisees in a difficult position: is it acceptable

---

1    See A. J. Levine, "Bearing False Witness: Common Errors Made about Early Judaism," in *The Jewish Annotated New Testament: Second Edition* (Oxford: Oxford University Press, 2017), 759–63.
2    See CD XI, 13–14A; 4Q265, frg. 7, I, 6–7.

to do "work" to rescue an animal but wrong to heal a person? Luke tells us, ". . . they could not reply to this" (Luke 14:6).

Yet, compared to others, the Pharisees could be perceived as wise and even lenient interpreters of the Scriptures. Ancient writers tell us that they were recognized for their devotion to God and, on account of this, were widely respected by the people. The first-century Jewish historian Josephus tells us, ". . . so great is their influence with the masses that even when they speak against a king or high priest, they immediately gain credibility."[3]

In light of all of this, it seems strange that Jesus faces opposition from Pharisees. On various points, Jesus and the Pharisees agreed. Unlike the Sadducees, another major Jewish group mentioned in the Gospels, the Pharisees upheld beliefs in the immortality of the soul, the existence of angels, and the resurrection of the dead (Acts 23:8)—all of which were affirmed by Jesus. Perhaps this is why it was easier for some of the Pharisees to become Jesus's followers (cf. Acts 15:5; cf. John 3:1; 19:39); nowhere in the New Testament do we hear of Sadducees later joining the Church. Jesus even says that the Pharisees "sit on Moses' seat; *so practice and observe whatever they tell you*" (Matthew 23:2–3).

### Paul the Pharisee and "Conversion"
One Pharisee who came to believe in Jesus was St. Paul. Paul writes,

> If anyone else has reason to be confident in the flesh, I have more: circumcised on the eighth day, a member of the people of Israel, of the tribe of Benjamin, a Hebrew born of Hebrews; *as to the law, a Pharisee; as to zeal, a persecutor of the church; as to righteousness under the law, blameless.* (Philippians 3:4–6)[4]

---

3  Josephus, *Antiquities of the Jews* 13.5 (288).
4  NRSV-CE slightly adapted.

As a Pharisee, Paul was genuinely committed to observing God's law and sought to be "blameless." There is no hint here of hypocrisy; as a Pharisee, Paul was sincerely zealous for the Scriptures of Israel (see also Acts 23:6; 26:5).

That said, Paul also came to believe these Scriptures can only be fully understood if one turns to Jesus. Paul makes this clear in 2 Corinthians 3. There he speaks of how the Israelites' "minds were hardened" at the time of Moses (2 Corinthians 3:14). Going on, he explains:

> ... to this day *whenever Moses is read a veil lies over their minds*; but *when a man turns to the Lord the veil is removed.* Now the Lord is the Spirit, and where the Spirit of the Lord is, there is freedom. And we all, with unveiled face, beholding the glory of the Lord, are being changed into his likeness from one degree of glory to another; for this comes from the Lord who is the Spirit. (2 Corinthians 3:15–18)

To be "changed" we must turn to the Lord. Only in beholding him and receiving the Spirit can we find true freedom. Without Christ, our minds remain hardened.

Yet turning *to* the Lord necessarily also means turning *away* from sin. Paul commends Gentile believers in Thessalonica because they had "turned to God from idols, to serve a living and true God" (1 Thessalonians 1:9). In the Vulgate, the Latin translation of the Bible used by the Church, the Greek word used for "turned" is rendered *conversi*, the term from which we get the English word "conversion." We might say, then, that *conversion* for Paul involves a twofold movement. On one hand, it involves a *turning from*, that is, it is a movement away from sin. On the other, it also entails a *turning to,* that is, a movement *towards* Christ. Both are essential: without turning from sin, we cannot turn to Christ, which is the only way the "veil" can be "removed."

### Blind Guides

The Gospels contain a similar message, teaching us that Christ comes to bring "light" to those in "darkness." In Matthew, we learn that Jesus fulfills Isaiah's prophecy: ". . . the people who sat in darkness have seen a great light" (Matthew 4:16; cf. Isaiah 9:2). In Luke, John the Baptist's father declared that God was about "to give light to those who sit in darkness" (Luke 1:79).

This theme is especially prominent in the Gospel according to John. In the first chapter, we read: "*The light shines in the darkness, and the darkness has not overcome it*" (John 1:5). Later, in John 8, Jesus therefore explains, "I am the light of the world; he who follows me will not walk in darkness, but will have the light of life" (John 8:12).

Jesus illustrates how he is the light of the world by healing a blind man. In doing this, Jesus explains that he has come into the world so "that those who do not see may see" (John 9:39). Yet there are Pharisees in the scene who refuse to believe. They ask derisively, "Are we also *blind?*" Jesus responds to them, ". . . now that you say, 'We see,' your guilt remains" (John 9:41). According to Jesus, these Pharisees were unable to see; they suffered from spiritual blindness.

The account coheres broadly with other reports in Matthew, Mark, and Luke in which Jesus castigates the religious leaders who oppose him due to their blindness. He warns that those who follow them will inevitably be led astray: "Let them alone; *they are blind guides. And if a blind man leads a blind man, both will fall into a pit*" (Matthew 15:14).

### The Tax Collector and the Pharisee

According to Jesus, impaired spiritual vision is rooted in an unwillingness to recognize one's own sinfulness. In the Gospel according to Luke, Jesus illustrates this by telling a parable in which a Pharisee serves as a kind of "anti-disciple."

Two men went up into the temple to pray, one a Pharisee and the other a tax collector. The Pharisee stood and prayed thus with himself, "God, I thank thee that I am not like other men, extortioners, unjust, adulterers, or even like this tax collector. I fast twice a week, I give tithes of all that I get." But the tax collector, standing far off, would not even lift up his eyes to heaven, but beat his breast, saying, "God, be merciful to me a sinner!" I tell you, this man went down to his house justified rather than the other; for every one who exalts himself will be humbled, but he who humbles himself will be exalted. (Luke 18:10–14)

Luke tells us that this parable addressed those who "*trusted in themselves that they were righteous and despised others*" (Luke 18:9). In the parable, the Pharisee represents such a person—he seems to trust in himself.

It is hard for us today to recognize the astonishing nature of this teaching, which casts the *tax collector* as a model for prayer. As we have discussed above, tax collectors were known as traitors to their people. They were also known to engage in corrupt practices. With all of this in mind we can better appreciate how surprising Jesus's Parable of the Tax Collector and Pharisee would have been in its original setting. Pharisees were honored and tax collectors were disdained. Yet Jesus holds out the latter as the model for prayer.

What makes the tax collector a better exemplar of prayer than the Pharisee in Jesus's parable? The Pharisee focuses on his good deeds, keeping a mental tally of them. He also indulges in spiritual pride by comparing himself to others (e.g., "I am not like . . . this tax collector"). The tax collector, however, spends no time thinking about the sins of others. He is focused on the problem *of his own sinfulness*. In fact, he is *acutely* aware of his sin. Instead of extolling his own virtues, he humbles himself, beseeching God for mercy.

The lesson is unmistakable: being self-righteous is *worse* than being a repentant tax collector. The two men embody the two figures identified by Jesus in the closing line: ". . . for every one who exalts himself will be humbled, but he who humbles himself will be exalted" (Luke 18:14).

### *Hypocrisy as a Universal Problem*

Spiritual blindness involves failing to see things correctly—especially one's own sinfulness. In one well-known passage, Jesus employs an exaggerated image to drive home this point:

> Why do you see the speck that is in your brother's eye, but do not notice the log that is in your own eye? Or how can you say to your brother, "Brother, let me take out the speck that is in your eye," when you yourself do not see the log that is in your own eye? You hypocrite, first take the log out of your own eye, and then you will see clearly to take out the speck that is in your brother's eye. (Luke 6:41–42)

This saying, however, is not targeted at the Pharisees. It is aimed at *all* who refuse to acknowledge their own sinfulness, most especially his disciples. Even *Peter* turns out to be a hypocrite, professing Jesus as Messiah (Mark 8:29) and promising to die with him if necessary (Mark 14:31), before denying that he even knows Jesus (Mark 14:66–72).

The Pharisees who opposed Jesus, then, were not uniquely guilty of self-righteousness—Jesus's disciples were too. The message we should take away from Jesus's critique of the Pharisees is not that they were somehow specially depraved. Rather, his point is this: if *even* the Pharisees failed to recognize their sin, no one is immune to spiritual blindness. The *Catechism* sums up Jesus's teaching this way: ". . . since sin is universal, those who pretend not to need salvation are blind to themselves" (*Catechism* §588).

## HARDEN NOT YOUR HEARTS

Coming to terms with our own sin is not easy. In the New Testament, we learn why: St. Paul teaches that due to Adam's disobedience, sin gained dominion over humanity. All are under the power of sin. As a product of that, we consistently refuse to take responsibility for our sinfulness. According to Genesis, this has been a problem from the very beginning.

### *Refusal to Repent in the Garden*
Most people are familiar with the basic outline of the story of Adam and Eve's failure in the garden. What is often forgotten is what happened *after* they consumed the forbidden fruit. The narrative offers us important insights into the nature of sin.

After Adam and Eve sin, God comes to them and asks, "Have you eaten of the tree of which I commanded you not to eat?" (Genesis 3:11). Adam responds by shamelessly "passing the buck": "The *woman* whom *thou gavest to be with me*, she gave me fruit of the tree, and I ate" (Genesis 3:12). With this answer, Adam manages to blame not only the woman, but also *God*. In effect, Adam says to his Creator: "*You* are to blame for my sin since *you* gave me this woman and put her here with me."

When God turns to Eve, she is no more willing to own up to what she has done than Adam. She responds, "The serpent beguiled me" (Genesis 3:13). Instead of confessing her guilt, Eve also points the finger at someone else, namely, the serpent. She claims that he "beguiled" her, that is, tricked her. In essence, Eve protests, "It is not *my* fault that I sinned!"

In the New Testament, Paul teaches that the sin committed in the garden marked a decisive moment in salvation history. He explains that Adam's action not only ushered sin into the world, it also caused all to be placed under its dominion. In his letter to the church at Rome, Paul insists, ". . . sin came into the world through one man" (Romans 5:12), adding, *"by one man's disobedience many were made sinners"* (Romans 5:19). Because of the sin of Adam, Paul teaches that "sin reigned" (Romans 5:21) and caused humanity to be "enslaved to sin" (Romans 6:6), a state he calls being "under sin" (Romans 7:14).

### Fallen Nature

Catholic teaching describes this state of fallen humanity as "original sin." The *Catechism* describes it as "the 'reverse side' of the Good News that Jesus is the Savior of all men, that all need salvation, and that salvation is offered to all through Christ" (§389). In other words, *salvation means reversing the effects of sin.*

In Romans, Paul does not simply speak about humanity's fallen condition in abstract terms. He offers a vivid account of what the struggle with sin looks like "on the ground":

> I do not understand my own actions. For I do not do what I want, but I do the very thing I hate. . . . For I know that nothing good dwells within me, that is, in my flesh. I can will what is right, but I cannot do it. For I do not do the good I want, but the evil I do not want is what I do. . . . Wretched man that I am! Who will deliver me from this body of death? (Romans 7:15, 18–19, 24)

Because of sin's hold on humanity, doing the good is not simply challenging, it is impossible.

The perilous situation humanity finds itself in should not be minimized. According to Paul, on its own power, human nature is incapable of doing what is required of it. Not only are our wills weakened so that we become unable to *choose* rightly, our minds are also affected by sin—we cannot even fully *understand* our own actions. Earlier in this same epistle, Paul talks about how sin causes human beings to become "futile in their thinking" so that "their senseless minds were darkened" (Romans 1:21). To put it bluntly, according to Paul, sin not only makes us weak, sin also makes us stupid, or at least foolish. Sin affects our minds and wills. Humanity, according to Paul, needs a "deliverer" (Romans 7:24).

### *The Heart of Sin*

According to the Bible, then, the problem of sin cannot be solved through self-help or firm resolutions. Sin runs deep. How deep? Scripture maintains that it even reaches our "hidden center," the heart (*Catechism* §2563). The prophet Jeremiah tells us, "The heart is deceitful above all things, and desperately corrupt; who can understand it?" (Jeremiah 17:9).

We would prefer not to think our situation is so dire. We like to congratulate ourselves on being "good people." Moreover, like Adam and Eve, we tend to resist taking ownership of our sins. We try to distance ourselves from them. To do that we come up with any number of excuses, including,

- "That isn't really who I am."
- "It's not a big deal."
- "I didn't hurt anyone."
- "I didn't mean anything by it."

Instead of saying, "I committed a sin," we choose to confess something far less damning: "I made a mistake."

But the biblical authors challenge us to confront ourselves with our sins. It is not a "mistake" to lie, cheat, steal, or hurt others knowingly. We *choose* to do these things. Recognizing this, the Church teaches us to confess our guilt. At Mass, we say a prayer in which we beat our breasts and state that we have sinned "through my fault, through my fault, through my most grievous fault."

Ironically, while we often fail to come to terms with our own sinfulness, we are quick to judge others. We readily and eagerly express moral outrage at the public downfall of a prominent figure, a coworker, a family member, a neighbor, etc. When it comes to the sins of others, we have great moral clarity, but when it comes to our own failings we even begin to wonder, "Is that really a sin?"

Suffice it to say, Paul did not take sin lightly. He compiled lists of various sins and condemned them outright. Consider Romans 1. There "murder" is mentioned alongside other vices such as "strife," "deceit," "gossip," and being "disobedient to parents" (Romans 1:29–32). When we think of sin, we can easily be tempted to think in terms of sins we have not committed. The sin of "murder" is easy to condemn if you have not committed it.

But are we deceitful? Do we sow seeds of discord in our families and workplaces? Do we talk about others behind their backs by slandering them? Are we guilty of detraction, that is, do we speak about the failings or weaknesses of others freely and without necessity? Do we bring dishonor to our parents? When we are confronted with these sins, do we simply shrug off our responsibility? Paul certainly did not.

Here is a good place to also mention the seven deadly sins recognized by Catholic tradition: anger, envy, vanity, avarice, lust, gluttony, sloth (cf. *Catechism,* §1866). We would do well to consider how we may have succumbed to these temptations. With God's grace, we must fight against the temptation to make excuses for their presence in our lives.

## THE NEED FOR SUPERNATURAL VISION

Because sin blinds us, we often fail to recognize our own brokenness. In the Gospel according to John, this is a lesson Jesus teaches a Pharisee named Nicodemus. As Nicodemus discovers, only in encountering Christ can we fully recognize the way sin impairs our outlook. Only in him can we find a new way to live.

### Jesus and Nicodemus

The story of Nicodemus's encounter with Jesus, which is found at the beginning of John 3, is set up nicely by the final verses of John 2. The Gospel writer highlights the limitations of humanity, described simply as "man":

> Now when he was in Jerusalem at the Passover feast, many believed in his name when they saw the signs which he did; but Jesus did not trust himself to them, because he knew all *men* and needed no one to bear witness of *man*; for he himself knew what was in *man*. (John 2:23–25)

Though many believed in Jesus, they did so in a deficient way; they only believed in him on the basis of what they could see him do. Those who believe in Jesus in this way only rely on their physical senses. Later, Jesus will speak of a faith that does not rely on what is seen: "Blessed are those who have not seen and yet believe" (John 20:29).

In other words, those who believe in Jesus merely because of what they can see do not have *supernatural faith*—they are not "blessed." Because of this, their "faith" is deficient. They are not trustworthy.

When Nicodemus is introduced at the beginning of John 3, he is presented as "exhibit A" of the untrustworthy "man." Picking up on themes that concluded the previous chapter, the evangelist writes,

> *Now there was a man* of the Pharisees, named Nicodemus, a ruler of the Jews. This *man* came to Jesus by night and said to him, "Rabbi, we know that you are a teacher come from God; for *no one can do these signs that you do, unless God is with him.*" (John 3:1–2)

Nicodemus only believes on account of Jesus's miracles. His faith is not a supernatural faith.

Let me underscore an important point: *Nicodemus's spiritual problem is not the result of being Pharisee.* He fails to understand not because he is a Pharisee, but because he is "a man." As John has already told us, Jesus "knew what was in *man*" (John 2:25). Even a Pharisee is not immune from the deficiencies of fallen human nature.

In responding to Nicodemus, Jesus uses a notable word, *anōthen*, which for now I will leave untranslated: "Amen, amen, I say to you, unless one is born *anōthen* he cannot see the kingdom of God" (John 3:3).[5] The term *anōthen* can mean either "again" or "from above." The entire meaning of Jesus's statement hangs on how one interprets the Greek term *anōthen*. You might think that knowing Greek would help you here but even knowing biblical languages does not necessarily clear things up. Why? Because Jesus has done something remarkable; he has chosen a word that has at least *two* meanings. Apart from context, it is not clear *which* meaning Jesus intends.

Jesus uses the word *anōthen* to show Nicodemus that his mind is set on worldly things. Nicodemus's response is remarkably revealing. He immediately thinks Jesus must be talking about a *physical* birth. Upon hearing that a man must be born *anōthen* to enter the kingdom of heaven, the Pharisee inquires: "How can a man be born when he is old? Can he enter a second time into his mother's womb and be born?" (John 3:4).

This response is comical. Surely Nicodemus cannot think that Jesus is suggesting people literally climb back into their mothers' wombs. Yet this is where Nicodemus's mind takes

---

5   RSV-CE slightly adapted.

him. The possibility that Jesus is using the term spiritually does not even occur to him.

The Fourth Gospel indicates that Nicodemus was a good and earnest man. When other Jerusalem leaders begin to scheme to destroy Jesus, Nicodemus speaks up against them: "Does our law judge a man without first giving him a hearing and learning what he does?" (John 7:51). Moreover, at the end of the Gospel he is listed with the disciples who prepare his body for burial (John 19:39). Yet, despite all of this, *even* Nicodemus is unable to think in a supernatural way.

### *The Blind Leading the Blind*

Jesus goes on to tell Nicodemus, ". . . unless one is born of water and the Spirit, he cannot enter the kingdom of God" (John 3:5). The context strongly suggests this is a reference to Baptism. Immediately after his conversation with Nicodemus, Jesus spends time with the disciples while they baptize: "After this Jesus and his disciples went into the land of Judea; there *he remained with them and baptized*" (John 3:22). This scene in John 3 is the only time in all of the Gospels where Jesus is present while his disciples are baptizing.[6] It is hard to believe this is mere coincidence. John deliberately connects Jesus's teaching about the need to be born with water and Spirit to a scene involving Baptism.

Moreover, by speaking of "water" and "Spirit," Jesus draws on imagery associated with the scene of his own Baptism, which seems to be alluded to earlier (cf. John 1:23–34). As John is baptizing with "water," he sees the "Spirit" descend on Jesus. From all of this, I think we can conclude—as Church fathers like Augustine did—that the spiritual rebirth in John 3 is depicted as a *sacramental* event.[7]

---

6   John later clarifies, "Jesus himself did not baptize, but only his disciples" (John 4:2).

7   See Augustine, *Tractates on the Gospel of John*, 11.4, 6. Though not all scholars are convinced that John 3:5 contains a baptismal reference, the contextual clues make it difficult to deny.

One important feature about Baptism that is often overlooked is that it signifies the way salvation occurs through Christ's working in others; you cannot baptize *yourself.* Salvation is *ecclesial,* that is, it is experienced through the ministry of the *Church* (the Greek word for "Church" is *ekklēsia*). Salvation is not merely an individualistic reality.

Since we are often unable to recognize our sins, the saints down through the ages have highlighted the need to develop virtuous friendships that are anchored in a mutual commitment to Christ. Jesus condemned "blind guides" because they are especially dangerous. They prey on a very real spiritual need, namely, that we require others to help hold us accountable. St. Francis de Sales writes, "For those who live in the world and desire to embrace true virtue it is necessary to unite together in holy, sacred friendship." [8]

What is more, the great spiritual masters of Catholic tradition—such as St. Francis de Sales, St. John of the Cross, and St. Teresa of Avila—recommend consulting with a spiritual advisor often. St. John of the Cross said, "The virtuous soul that is alone and without a master is like a burning coal; it will grow colder rather than hotter."[9] He went on, "The blind person who falls will not be able to get up alone; the blind person who does get up alone will go off on the wrong road."[10] It is especially helpful to find a priest who can hear our confessions regularly. By getting to know us well, such a priest can attain a helpful perspective on our struggles and aid our spiritual growth.

We each must come face-to-face with our own sinfulness. We need to confront ourselves (and be confronted by others) with sins we fail to acknowledge, especially the ones to which

---

8  *Introduction to the Devout Life,* III.19.
9  St. John of the Cross, "The Sayings of Light and Love," no. 7. Taken from St. John of the Cross, *The Collected Works of St. John of the Cross,* 3d ed. (Washington, D.C.: Institute of Carmelite Studies Publications, 2017), 86.
10  Ibid., no. 11; *Collected Works,* 86.

we might be blind. Christ speaks to us through other people—but we must be willing to listen. This involves a constant process of spiritual growth. As Jesus warned, if we say, "we see," we are blind. We must heed his advice and recognize that we must *"first take the log out of your own eye"* (Matthew 7:5).

When I was first asked if I was saved, I was offended. I have learned how wrong I was to have that reaction to the question. If we do not think we need salvation, we cannot receive it. Salvation is not merely "for other people." Like Mary, each one of us must recognize that God is "my savior." We all have logs in our own eyes that we choose to ignore. We cannot recognize them apart from Christ. He often points them out to us by working through other people. Are we willing to listen to him?

**10**

# Not Merely about the Future

We know that the whole creation has been groaning in travail together until now; and not only the creation, but we ourselves, who have the first fruits of the Spirit, groan inwardly as we wait for adoption as sons, the redemption of our bodies.

—Romans 8:22–23

Christians are called to be the light of the world. Thus, the Church shows forth the kingship of Christ over all creation and in particular over human societies.

—*Catechism of the Catholic Church* §2105

Street preachers and signs held up at sporting events regularly remind us that Jesus *died* for our salvation. This is true. As we have seen, the cross is an essential dimension of Jesus's work of redemption.

What often gets overlooked is that Jesus also *rose* in order to save us. Paul is emphatic—the resurrection is essential. He writes, ". . . if Christ has not been raised, then our preaching is in vain and your faith is in vain" (1 Corinthians 15:14). The Apostle even states that Jesus was "put to death for our trespasses and *raised for our justification*" (Romans 4:25).

If we make the resurrection just an "epilogue" to Christ's work of redemption, we fail to appreciate what salvation truly means. Salvation is more than just the salvation of our "souls." Salvation in Christ is not merely about immaterial and incorporeal realities. Nor is it simply about dealing with the consequences of sin. Salvation is ordered to resurrection and transformation. This involves not only a spiritual dimension but a physical one as well. Nevertheless, sharing in the risen life of Christ is something believers already experience *in this life.*

## THE RESURRECTION AND A NEW CREATION

In the New Testament, Jesus's resurrection is not the "end" of the story—it truly is a new beginning. In this, the New Testament writers draw on ancient Jewish hopes for a new creation. In this, Jesus's work of redemption has a sacramental nature.

### *The Resurrection and the Age to Come*

The New Testament authors speak of the way Christ's work has ushered in a "new creation" or a "new age." Consider some of the following passages:

> [God] raised [Christ] from the dead and made him sit at his right hand in the heavenly places, far above all rule and authority and power and dominion, and above every name that is named, *not only in this age but also in that which is to come.* (Ephesians 1:20–21)

> Grace to you and peace from God the Father and our Lord Jesus Christ, who gave himself for our sins to deliver us from *the present evil age,* according to the will of our God and Father, to whom be the glory for *the age of ages.* Amen. (Galatians 1:3–5)[1]

> For *the form of this world is passing away.* (1 Corinthians 7:31)

---

1    RSV-CE slightly adapted.

> . . . if anyone is in Christ, he is *a new creation*; the old has passed
> away, behold, *the new has come*. (2 Corinthians 5:17)

The language here is steeped in Jewish traditions.

The promise of a "new creation" is rooted in the Old
Testament prophetic books. The book of Isaiah, for example,
concludes with a vision of the coming of a "new heavens" and
"new earth" (Isaiah 66:22). Out of such texts, later Jewish
sources developed a conception of "two ages" or "two worlds,"
the present age/world and the age/world to come. The New
Testament authors represent some of the earliest witnesses to
this tradition.[2]

Jewish hopes for a new world/creation were also closely
tied to belief in the resurrection from the dead. For example,
in the book of Daniel, we read about how the righteous will
not only be raised from the dead, they will also be glorified:

> And many of those who sleep in the dust of the earth shall
> awake, some to *everlasting life* [literally: "the life of the age"],
> and some to shame and everlasting contempt. And those who
> are wise shall shine like the brightness of the firmament; and
> those who turn many to righteousness, like the stars for ever and
> ever. (Daniel 12:2–3)

Daniel goes on to connect this vision to "the time of the end"
(Daniel 12:4). Based on such hopes, many Jews believed that
God's final vindication of the righteous would involve resurrection
(see also 2 Maccabees 7:22–23; Wisdom 2:23; 3:4–7).

In short, since God is the Creator, Jewish tradition affirmed
that the ultimate redemption of God's people would trump
even death. God would bring about a new creation. This
would involve nothing less than resurrection from the dead.

---

2    See Pitre, Barber, and Kincaid, *Paul*, chapter 2.

### Jesus's Resurrection as First Fruits

The New Testament's teaching about Christ's resurrection draws together these Jewish traditions. Jesus's resurrection is the in-breaking of the new age. Moreover, in line with Jewish hopes, the New Testament writers affirm that there will be a resurrection of all the dead at the end of time that will involve glorification.

The Gospel writers all report that Jesus himself announced the day of a future resurrection of the dead involving some sort of transformation. For example, Jesus says, "For when they rise from the dead, they neither marry nor are given in marriage, but are *like angels in heaven*" (Mark 12:25). The Fourth Gospel also includes many references to the idea that those who die in Christ will rise again and be given "eternal life" (cf. John 5:28–29; 6:54; etc.). Of course, Jesus's resurrection is the model for understanding all of this.

On the one hand, the Gospel accounts are clear that Jesus's resurrection includes an actual *material* dimension; he remains "flesh and bones" (Luke 24:39). Jesus shows the disciples that his resurrected body is no mirage. He displays to them the marks from his wounds and asks to be given food to eat in order to prove that he is no "ghost" or "spirit" (Luke 24:39–42; John 20:19–29).

Nevertheless, Jesus's body is also *changed.* He is somehow able to vanish quickly from sight (Luke 24:31). He even passes through locked doors (John 20:19). Recognizing this, Catholic teaching maintains, "Christ's Resurrection was not a return to earthly life, as was the case with the raisings from the dead that he had performed before Easter . . . In his risen body he passes from the state of death to another life beyond time and space (*Catechism* §646).

As we have seen, the goal of salvation is being conformed to the image of the Son. In the resurrection of believers, this is fully accomplished. Christ's resurrected body is, as St. Paul puts it, the "first fruits" of a coming harvest: "But in fact Christ has been raised from the dead, the first fruits of those who have fallen asleep. For as by a man came death, by a man has come also the resurrection of the dead. For as in Adam all die, so also in Christ shall all be made alive" (1 Corinthians 15:20–22).

The work of redemption affects the *whole* human person. This means that it is not only the soul that is to be saved. Resurrection is not merely the ascent of the soul to God. Nor is resurrection just the body coming "back to life." The hope of the resurrection involves sharing in the life to come in a bodily way that entails the glorification of the body.

### *A Sacramental Worldview*

Yet the New Testament departs from the Jewish outlook in one significant way: *the new age is not just a future reality.* With the resurrection of Christ, the new creation *has already dawned.* Believers are, in a way, standing with one foot in both the old and the new creation. Paul puts it this way:

> For the creation waits with eager longing for the revealing of the sons of God; for the creation was subjected to futility, not of its own will but by the will of him who subjected it in hope; because *the creation itself will be set free from its bondage to decay* and obtain the glorious liberty of the children of God. We know that *the whole creation has been groaning in travail together until now;* and not only the creation, but we ourselves, who have the first fruits of the Spirit, groan inwardly as we wait for adoption as sons, *the redemption of our bodies.* (Romans 8:19–23)

While awaiting the full realization of redemption, believers groan. They long not only for the redemption of their bodies but, in some way, for the redemption of the whole cosmos.

Pope Benedict and Pope Francis teach that creation cannot be detached from God's saving purposes within history. The world points beyond itself—it has sacramental significance.

Both popes appeal to Romans 1:20: "Ever since the creation of the world his invisible nature, namely, his eternal power and deity, has been clearly perceived in the things that have been made."[3] In addition, Benedict quotes Ephesians 1, which speaks of God's "plan for the fulness of time, to unite all things in [Christ], things in heaven and things on earth" (Ephesians 1:10). In Christ, Pope Benedict explains, "The cosmos finds its true meaning."[4]

This perspective is reflected in the Church's sacramental celebration. The material elements of nature—i.e., water, bread, wine, oil—are taken up into Christ's work. Pope Benedict XVI teaches that God brings about the new creation so that "through the things of the earth . . . we can communicate with him in a personal way."[5] The sacramental celebration of the resurrection is therefore "thanksgiving for the fact that God does not let creation be destroyed but restores it after all of man's attempts to destroy it."[6]

The popes teach that the world must never be detached from God's purpose for humanity. Using a term coined by Pope St. John Paul II, Pope Benedict XVI speaks of the need for a "human ecology," which recognizes the "covenant between human beings and the environment."[7] He insists:

> The book of nature is one and indivisible: it takes in not only the environment, but also life, sexuality, marriage, the family, social relations: in a word, integral human development. Our duties toward the environment are linked to our duties toward the human person, considered in himself and in relation to other.[8]

Salvation cannot simply be construed in spiritual terms.

---

3     See, e.g., Francis, *Laudato Si'*, Encyclical Letter (May 24, 2015), no. 12.
4     Joseph Ratzinger, *The Spirit of the Liturgy* (San Francisco: Ignatius, 2000), 108.
5     Ibid., 173.
6     Ibid., 96.
7     Benedict XVI, "Message for the Celebration of the World Day of Peace," no. 7.
8     Benedict XVI, Caritas in *Veritate*, Encyclical Letter (June 29, 2009), no. 51.

Those who are in Christ *must* work tirelessly to protect the poor and the oppressed. After all, as we have seen, according to Jesus's own teaching, the verdict we receive at the final judgment will depend upon whether we feed the hungry, give drink to the thirsty, welcome the stranger, clothe the naked, and visit the sick and imprisoned (Matthew 25:31–45). We do not love God in a disembodied way. This extends to showing care for the environment which is necessary for physical health and life.

Nevertheless, we must be careful not to fall into the trap of reducing the Gospel to building an earthly utopia. Nor should we care more about the world than the people who are in it. Salvation is not simply about a "this-worldly" kingdom of God. Victory over evil will not be realized on this side of Christ's second coming. Catholic teaching is emphatic on this point:

> The Church will enter the glory of the kingdom only through this final Passover, when she will follow her Lord in his death and Resurrection [cf. Revelation 19:1–9]. The kingdom will be fulfilled, then, not by a historic triumph of the Church through a progressive ascendancy, but only by God's victory over the final unleashing of evil, which will cause his Bride to come down from heaven. (*Catechism* §677)

Salvation, at the end of the day, is not fully attainable in this world; evil will only be defeated once and for all on the last day.

## RESURRECTION AND NEW LIFE

Though Christ's resurrection anticipates what will happen to all of the righteous on the last day, it also makes manifest that a new creation *has already been inaugurated*. The defeat of death on Easter Sunday signals Christ's ultimate victory over sin. The New Testament authors therefore explain that believers must live in accord with this truth.

### Putting Sin to Death

As we have seen, the effects of sin remain ever-present in this life. Paul states that even in this life sinners experience the punishment due to sin (Romans 1:27). Regret, pain, sadness, and broken families are only some of the ways this is made manifest. As Paul and other New Testament authors explain, as one descends into sin, one becomes addicted to its pleasures and enslaved to temptation.

In Christ, believers *already share in his resurrection.* This is first experienced in Baptism (Romans 6:3–4). Still, there also remains an unrealized dimension of salvation. This is specifically linked to the body in Romans. Paul tells us that we "groan" while "we wait for . . . the redemption of our bodies" (Romans 8:23).

In what way is the body "unredeemed"? For one thing, as we have seen, Paul suggests creation is awaiting the fullness of redemption inasmuch as it remains subject to death and decay. The body is therefore only entirely redeemed once it is fully conformed to Christ's risen body.

The unrealized dimension of redemption is also tied to another concept: our disordered passions. In Galatians, Paul explains, "For the desires of the flesh are against the Spirit, and the desires of the Spirit are against the flesh; for these are opposed to each other, to prevent you from doing what you would" (Galatians 5:17). Likewise, in Colossians we are told, "Put to death therefore what is earthly in you: immorality, impurity, passion, evil desire, and covetousness, which is idolatry. . . . In these you once walked, when you lived in them. But now put them all away" (Colossians 3:5, 7–8).

### Spiritual Training

To explain the struggle against our fallen humanity, Paul uses the analogy of a runner in training:

> Do you not know that in a race all the runners compete, but only one receives the prize? So run that you may obtain it. *Every athlete*

*exercises self-control* in all things. *They do it to receive a perishable wreath, but we an imperishable.* Well, I do not run aimlessly, I do not box as one beating the air; but *I pommel my body and subdue it, lest after preaching to others I myself should be disqualified.* (1 Corinthians 9:24–27)

To "run the race" of the Christian life successfully, one must learn to renounce one's own disordered desires like an athlete who trains for a race. Just as a champion runner must learn self-discipline, so too the Christian must learn "self-control in all things."

A similar image is found in 1 Timothy, where we read: "*Train* yourself in godliness; for while bodily training is of some value, godliness is of value in every way, as it holds promise for the present life and also for the life to come" (1 Timothy 4:7–8). The Christian life is therefore viewed as consisting of a kind of spiritual training consisting of self-discipline.

Early Christian writers referred to this kind of spiritual discipline as *askēsis*. Paul uses the verbal form of the term in Acts: "So I always take pains [Greek *askō*] to have a clear conscience before God and men" (Acts 24:16). As one scholar puts it, the word Paul uses "could apply to any regimen of exercise with a goal of improvement."[9] Clement of Alexandria compared Christian *askēsis* to the preparation of an Olympic athlete, who "for a long time subjected his body to thorough training in order to the attainment of manly strength."[10]

Over time, reflection on this idea developed into a specific branch of Catholic Spiritual Theology, known as Ascetical Theology, which reflects on practices like fasting. These acts involve "putting to death" the things of the flesh; they teach us how to renounce worldly desires. They are often referred to as "mortifications" (that is, "putting to death"). We enter

---

9   Teresa M. Shaw, *The Burden of the Flesh* (Minneapolis: Fortress, 1998), 5.

10   Clement of Alexandria, *Stomata*, 7.7.

into these practices together as members of Christ's body. The *Catechism* maintains that such actions are for all the faithful: "Spiritual progress entails the ascesis and mortification that gradually lead to living in the peace and joy of the Beatitudes" (§2015). These spiritual disciplines teach us how to share in the victory of the New Adam, Christ, who ushers in the new creation.

## SHARING IN THE NEW ADAM'S VICTORY OVER SATAN

As we have already examined, Paul teaches that sin entered into the world through the disobedience of Adam. Paul's logic indicates that, prior to sinning in the garden, humanity was not "under sin" (cf. Romans 7:14), that is, under its rule. After the fall, humanity became enslaved to sin's power. Yet Christ, the New Adam, succeeds where Adam failed.

The story of the fall of Adam and Eve, recounted in the book of Genesis, is well known. Most people, however, fail to pay attention to some of the most important details of the story. Indeed, Christian tradition has long found great significance in the specifics of the serpent's temptations. By looking at this story in light of the New Testament, we come to a deeper understanding of what Christ's victory entails— and how we can share in it.

### *The Fall and the Threefold Temptation*

As is well known, Adam and Eve eat of the forbidden fruit at the behest of the serpent, a figure the Bible later identifies as Satan (cf. Revelation 12:9). There is an interesting feature in the narrative that we can easily overlook: the forbidden fruit represented *a threefold temptation*. Here I will provide the text of Genesis but add numbers to make each element clear:

So when the woman saw that the tree was [1] *good for food*, and that [2] *it was a delight to the eyes*, and that the tree was [3] *to be desired to make one wise*, she took of its fruit and ate; and she also gave some to her husband, and he ate." (Genesis 3:6)

The *Catechism* links this episode to 1 John 2, which warns of three temptations. Again, I am adding numbers to specify the three items that are identified:

Do not love the world or the things in the world. If any one loves the world, love for the Father is not in him. For all that is in the world, [1] *the lust of the flesh* and [2] *the lust of the eyes* and [3] *the pride of life*, is not of the Father but is of the world. And the world passes away, and the lust of it; but he who does the will of God abides for ever. (1 John 2:15–17)

The *Catechism* uses this passage from 1 John to explain the effects of Adam's sin. Before succumbing to the tempter, Adam is said to have been *"free from the triple concupiscence"* described by 1 John (§377). Some key observations about all of this need to be made.

To begin with, by linking the temptations humanity faces described in 1 John to the fall, the *Catechism* shows us that the struggles we face today can be traced back to the garden. The temptations we encounter are essentially those to which Adam and Eve succumbed. Moreover, the *Catechism* indicates that the three temptations found in 1 John represent a kind of summary of all temptations. In this, the *Catechism* picks up an interpretive tradition that goes back to the early Church. St. Augustine, for example, wrote that the three vices mentioned "embrace all sins."[11]

What is more, the *Catechism* elaborates on what the threefold temptation consists of, namely, "the pleasures of the senses,

---

11   Exposition of Psalm 8, no. 13.

covetousness for earthly goods, and self-assertion, contrary to the dictates of reason" (§377). Let us break these down.

First, "the pleasures of the senses" correspond to 1 John's "lust of the flesh." Broadly, this would refer to illicit carnal desires, which include sexual immorality and sins involving abusive excess of food or drink, such as gluttony and drunkenness. It could also be seen as referring to other kinds of substance abuse whose appeal involves illicit physical pleasure. Second, the notion of "covetousness for earthly goods" describes the meaning of the "lust of the eyes." In ancient Jewish and Christian sources, sins associated with wealth and the accumulation of goods are linked with the notion of the temptation of the "eyes."[12] Finally, "self-assertion" would seem to describe what 1 John calls "the pride of life." This may be understood in terms of the desire to put oneself over others; it is the desire for power.

It is fitting, then, that the *Catechism's* teaching identifies the threefold lust with the fall. As John Bergsma and Brant Pitre observe, the three temptations associated with the forbidden fruit in Genesis can be viewed as paralleling the three temptations described by 1 John 2.[13]

| The Threefold Lust | Three Temptations | The Forbidden Fruit |
|---|---|---|
| "the lust of the flesh" | "pleasures of the senses" | "good for food" |
| "the lust of the eyes" | "covetousness for earthly goods" | "a delight to the eyes" |
| "the pride of life" | "self-assertion" | desirable "to make one wise" |

---

12    See W. D. Davies and Dale Allison, *Gospel According to Saint Matthew*, 3 vols., (London: T & T Clark, 1988, 1991, 1997), 1:640, who explain that the "evil eye" is "the antithesis of generosity."

13    See John Bergsma and Brant Pitre, *A Catholic Introduction to the Bible: The Old Testament* (San Francisco: Ignatius Press, 2018), 126–27.

In other words, the forbidden fruit was desirable as food; it appealed to the carnal desire, that is, "the lust of the flesh." It was also a "delight to the eyes," which corresponds to "the lust of the eyes." Finally, the fruit is said to impart knowledge of good and evil. As interpreters have observed, determining what is "good" is God's prerogative in the Genesis narrative—he pronounces created things "good" (Genesis 1) and recognizes that man's solitude is "not good" (Genesis 2:18). The serpent suggests if they just eat of the fruit, "you will be like God, knowing good and evil" (Genesis 3:5). This involves "self-assertion" in its most naked form; they are tempted with the promise that they can be like God without God.

## The New Adam's Triumph over Temptation

As we have seen, the New Testament indicates that Christ has ushered in a new creation. Though this happens in the resurrection, the Gospels highlight this idea in various ways. The prologue to the Fourth Gospel opens with the first words of Genesis, "In the beginning" (John 1:1). The first verse of the Gospel of Matthew uses the Greek term translated "Genesis": "The book of the genealogy [Greek *geneseōs*] of Jesus Christ" (Matthew 1:1). Likewise, the Gospel according to Luke explicitly traces Jesus's genealogy all the way back to Adam (Luke 3:38).

Against this backdrop, the temptation of Jesus in the wilderness—found in both Matthew and Luke—takes on greater significance. Where Adam fails, Christ succeeds. The *Catechism* explains that Jesus sums up "the temptations of Adam in Paradise" (§538, quoting Luke 4:13).

What did these temptations involve? Writers such as St. Augustine believed it was no coincidence that Matthew and Luke indicate that Jesus faced *three* temptations. Though they appear in a different order in the two Gospel accounts, the essence of the three temptations is the same in each. Let us follow Luke's chronology.

First, after fasting for forty days in the wilderness, Satan seeks to pounce on the weakness of Jesus's hunger, encouraging him to turn stones into bread. Second, Satan shows Jesus the "glory" of the kingdoms of the world and promises to give them to Jesus if he will only bow down and worship him. Third, Satan tells Jesus to throw himself down from the pinnacle of the temple, trusting that God will send the angels to bear him up.

St. Augustine points out that Luke concludes the narrative by telling us that the devil departed from Jesus only after he "had ended *every temptation*" (Luke 4:13). Augustine believes the three temptations Jesus faces in the wilderness can be viewed in connection with 1 John's discussion of the threefold lust. By facing a test involving each element of the threefold lust, the devil truly confronted Jesus with *every* temptation.

Inspired by this insight and following the *Catechism's* explanation of the threefold lust, we can see a certain symmetry here between the account of the fall, 1 John's enumeration of vice, and the three temptations of Jesus. First, by renouncing the desire to satisfy his hunger, Jesus overcomes a temptation involving carnal appetites. Second, in renouncing the glory of the worldly kingdoms—a notion associated with wealth—Christ overcomes the lust of the eyes. Finally, in refusing to cast himself down and rely on the angels to bear him up, Christ refuses to assert himself, thereby conquering the pride of life.

### Jesus's Prescription for the New Creation

But Jesus does not only teach by his actions in the four Gospels. In Matthew's Gospel, the account of Jesus's temptation in the wilderness gives way immediately to the Sermon on the Mount. Here Jesus talks about three specific spiritual disciplines. In each case, Jesus warns that these must not be done in order to gain praise from others. Nevertheless, Jesus indicates that he expects his disciples to practice them.

... when you give alms, do not let your left hand know what your right hand is doing, so that your alms may be in secret; and your Father who sees in secret will reward you.

... when you pray, go into your room and shut the door and pray to your Father who is in secret; and your Father who sees in secret will reward you.

... when you fast, anoint your head and wash your face, that your fasting may not be seen by men but by your Father who is in secret; and your Father who sees in secret will reward you. (Matthew 6:3–4, 6, 17–18)

Notice that Jesus does not say "*if* you give alms," "*if* you pray," or "*if* you fast." Instead, he assumes that his disciples will carry out these disciplines as a matter of course.

Why does Jesus choose *these* activities? John Bergsma and Brant Pitre highlight the way fasting, almsgiving, and prayer seem to align with the threefold temptation of the forbidden fruit, the threefold lust described by 1 John, and the three temptations Jesus faces in the wilderness.[14] In fasting, disciples battle against the lust of flesh. Through almsgiving, believers learn to renounce worldly goods. Finally, in prayer, one subjects oneself to the will of God and overcomes the tendency of self-assertion.

| The Threefold Lust (1 John 2:16) | The Forbidden Fruit (Genesis 3:6) | The Temptations in the Wilderness | Three Spiritual Disciplines |
|---|---|---|---|
| "the lust of the flesh" | "good for food" | satisfy hunger | fasting |
| "the lust of the eyes" | "a delight to the eyes" | receive the glory of the kingdoms | almsgiving |
| "the pride of life" | desirable "to make one wise" | call upon angelic intervention | prayer |

---

14    See Bergsma and Pitre, *A Catholic Introduction*, 126–27.

Through fasting, almsgiving, and prayer one can be more closely conformed to the New Adam and, in him, overcome the fallen world and its temptations as he did.

Salvation is not merely a future reality awaiting us only in heaven. The new life of the new creation involves overcoming sin through the grace of union with Christ *even now.* This involves more than lofty ideals. It is nothing less than entering into spiritual battle with the enemy.

Winning the battle means overcoming impossible odds. Nevertheless, Christ himself promises his disciples, "With God all things are possible" (Matthew 19:26). Whatever temptation we are called to battle, then, we should never despair. For each of us, the battle is different. It may seem that freedom from a particular vice is unattainable, but never forget this—the voice telling you that you cannot change comes from the tempter. Faith means trusting not in our own righteousness or even our own capacity for it but trusting instead in the divine Son.

A final note. We can apply this lesson not only individually but communally. We may despair at scandals we hear about in the Church. True reform may seem impossible. Again, beware the tempter. Rather than succumbing to the despair and apathy to which the tempter seeks to lead us, let us instead embrace God's call to share in Christ's sonship and participate in his work of redemption, assured that "the power at work within us is able to do *far more abundantly than all that we ask or think,* to him be glory *in the church and in Christ Jesus* to all generations, for ever and ever. Amen" (Ephesians 3:20–21). Transformation is possible, but only to those who trust in him. The question we must ask is: do we trust him?

# ACKNOWLEDGEMENTS

This book would never have been possible had it not been for the support and generosity of many people. I owe deep appreciation to all the people at the Augustine Institute who helped make this project a reality. I thank Tim Gray for believing in this book and encouraging me to work on it. In addition, I thank my colleagues on the faculty of the Augustine Institute Graduate School, in particular, Christopher Blum, Mark Giszczak, Ben Akers, Elizabeth Klein, Douglas Bushman, Tim Herrman, Scott Hefelfinger, and Lucas Pollice. Although I had long wanted to write a book on the nature of salvation in Scripture, it was a particularly important conversation at a faculty meeting that provided the impetus for this project. In various ways, all of those professors shaped the presentation here. I also extend my thanks to Joseph Pearce for his encouragement and editorial help on this project. Furthermore, I also wish to express appreciation to Grace Hagan's copy edits, which saved me from multiple embarrassments, and Ben Dybas, who worked patiently on the book's fine cover design. I owe an especially profound debt of gratitude to Brant Pitre, John Kincaid, and John Sehorn who pored over the manuscript and offered invaluable feedback and corrections that significantly improved it. I am profoundly grateful for their generosity of spirit, advice, and, most of all, for their friendship. I am particularly grateful to Brant for his gracious Foreword. I also thank Andrew Swafford for carefully proofreading the manuscript and for offering suggestions that strengthened it. Of course, the deficiencies of this book are solely attributable to me.

I also thank my parents, Patrick and Theresa, for their constant encouragement and prayers. Furthermore, I thank my uncle, Fr. Peter Irving, for an important conversation that helped convince me that the book should be a priority.

Whenever a family man works on a project like this one, it is a group effort. I am, therefore, deeply grateful to my children, Michael, Matthew, Molly, Thomas, Susanna, and Simon for all the love you have shown to me and your patience with me. Above all, words fail to properly communicate my gratitude to my wife, Kimberly, for all she did to support me during the writing process. Her encouragement, patience, and love made this book possible.

Finally,

> With my mouth I will give great thanks to the LORD;
>> I will praise him in the midst of the throng.
> For he stands at the right hand of the needy,
>> to save him from those who condemn him to death.
>
> (Psalm 109:30–31)

# SUBJECT INDEX

# SCRIPTURE INDEX

# ONE YEAR.
# 20 MINUTES A DAY.

Encounter the Power and
Wonder of God's Word with
*Bible in a Year.* The simple
format guides you through all
73 books of the Bible in just one year.

Learn more at **CatholicBibleInAYear.com**